1

Steven Neary's Tips For A Good Life

By

Mark Neary

This book is dedicated to August and Mr B, two wonderful friends who know how to keep a blocked author's pecker up.

Introduction

Sometimes when I'm telling the Get Steven Home story at a public event, I take requests. During the Q&A, someone might stick their hand up and say, "Can you tell us the balcony and the risk assessment folder story?" This book came to life following a request. I tweeted a story from my blog and someone replied asking to see a compilation of some of Steven's best stories. That's what this book is. Think of it as a Now That's What I Call Steven Neary.

Back in 2010, my autistic son Steven went away for three days respite after I went down with flu and the local authority kept him away from home for 358 days. Their plan was to send him even further away to a long term placement in Wales. It was a race against time to stop that happening. After many setbacks we finally got to the Court of Protection and two hours into the hearing the judge ruled that Steven could return home immediately. Six months later we returned to court where the judge examined the legality of the council's actions. He ruled that all four deprivation of liberty authorisations that had been served on Steven were unlawful and that throughout the year his Article 5 Human Rights (Right to liberty) and his Article 8 Human Rights (Right to a private and family life) had been breached.

The court case catapulted Steven and I into the public eye. All the broadsheets covered the story and lots of television and radio programmes wanted to hear about the experience. Eight years on and I'm still invited to tell the story at all manner of public events.

A year after Steven came home, I started to write a blog. One of the things I found hardest about Steven's year away was the way the local authority presented Steven in their voluminous care records and the court reports. They turned him into an object. A negative specimen under a microscope. There was certainly no sense of the stoic, funny, uncomplicated, unique man that I spend my life with. I vowed to present the fully dimensional Steven and try and help him take his place in the world. A blog, writing about the day to day stuff seemed to be the best vehicle for this ambition. It became apparent very quickly that the readers liked Steven's world view. They admired the way he structures his life and chuckled at the way he cuts through all the nonsense that most of us become tangled up in. This book is a collection of the stories I have narrated over the last six years.

In 2018 I was involved in the online exhibition Rightful Lives. The project came about after a string of high profile cases showed that autistic people and people with learning disabilities are seen by the system that is meant to serve them as not quite human. Thousands of learning disabled people are trapped in dire situations and yet the Human Rights Act barely touches their lives. One of the aims of the exhibition was to pose and examine the question – why might that be? As curators, we determined to show the humanness of this group of people, creating and living their lives in thoroughly unique fashion. And to compare those lives with many other learning disabled people who have absolutely no say whatsoever in how they live their life. I like to think the end result of the exhibition (in which Steven contributed) presented many different creative lives, full of the normal stuff of life: hopes, dreams, interests, frustrations, sadness, humour, talents and much much more.

The parents of people with learning disabilities are sometimes criticised for speaking on behalf of their children. Of taking away their agency, no matter how good their intentions. I'm sure it occasionally happens and it's something that I reflect on every time I write about Steven. With this book am I promoting his voice or taking it away? Every quote I use are his words. I try to avoid analysing him or trying to understand what is behind his words. I try to tell his stories as phenomenalogically as I can. At the same time though, I'm aware that if Steven was able to write this book himself it would probably be a very different story. I'm sure he would tell his same jokes because he likes to see people laugh and I think he's proud of his ability to construct a joke. On the other hand I've included some stories because they make me laugh where the humour comes from the straightforwardness of Steven's communication and the bemusement or discomfort of the person on the receiving end. The joke is never on Steven though. I also don't tend to write about his discomforts – his anxieties, his meltdowns, his traumas because that isn't my place to do. If I've learned nothing else as a counsellor, it is to be respectful of others' boundaries. So this book may not be his story. Or my story. But a story from that special place where our lives join through love and shared experiences.

I have deliberately not presented the chapters in chronological order. Whilst it is true that Steven has matured massively in the last six years the point of the book is not about someone's growth. Once again, that would feel presumptuous and could easily detract from his voice and experience. I wanted his wisdom to drive the narrative and that doesn't need a binary timeline. Steven has an interesting relationship with time and it felt right for this book to reflect that. He sees himself as "an orderly man" and a story from 1998 can carry as much potency as a story from last month when he recounts it.

I've also rejected the idea of categorising the stories. I set out to and originally collated all the references to pop music into one section. But then I scrapped that idea, realising again that I was imposing a structure that was more mine than his. One of the delights of living with Steven is when the real world and a fictional world merge as one. The local newsagent and Basil Fawlty can appear in the same narrative and in Steven's eyes there is no distinction between the two. This means there is a complete randomness in the order of the chapters but Steven enjoys keeping people on their toes.

This book is not a story about autism or learning disability. You may not learn anything about either state. You may recognise some minor detail but that is that.

It's basically the story (and I know I'm biased) of a man with some pretty interesting things to say.

Enrique – I'm Trying To Get Some Sleep In Here

June 5, 2013

4.45 This morning.

My bedroom door flies open and Steven comes in with one of his most quizzical looks:

"Dad. It was Enrique's first song called?........"

"Bailamos Steve".

Steven starts singing with huge grin.

"Enrique does marvellous singing Dad".

"He does Steve. Now go back to bed, we've got Mr Bean in the morning".

Steven gets to the door and turns back:

"Dad. Bailamos is a?.............."

Shit. I should have seen this coming. This is Steven's way of phrasing the question, "What does Bailamos mean?". A quick response is needed; it will take too long to switch on the computer and search a Google translation.

I take a shot in the dark.

"Is Bailamos a thing?"

"Dad's talking silly. Bailamos is a dance".

I'm caught between needing to go back to sleep and curiosity. Thankfully Steven comes to the rescue.

"Bailamos is MFL talking Dad"

Having learned that they covered Enrique in modern foreign languages at school, we could now get back to sleep for another hour.

A Bit of Jip

Good news. After weeks of being passed from pillar to post trying to arrange Steven's blood test, yesterday I thought I'd have one last bash at appealing to the practice manager at our surgery. To my surprise, Steven's GP had only returned that day from long term sick leave and I was put through to her. She is great. Within a couple of hours she called me back to say that she'd arranged for the senior male partner in the practice to do the bloods on Friday morning. Fantastic, human empathic service. Now to prepare Steven.....

When he was younger, Steven was completely thrown by pain. He didn't have the language so it was all expressed in distressing behaviour. And he would never allow anyone to attend to him. If he picked a scab, he would hide himself away and later we'd find the hall curtains covered in blood. Thankfully, Basil Fawlty entered his life. Steven had a word. Jip. So now, he can say what and where he has a problem – "Dad – got a bit of jip in my back". Much easier to deal with.

Then along came Holby City. Steven loves a regular ensemble cast, so it soon became favourite viewing. The script is so formulaic that you can wager your house that every Tuesday at 20.40, they perform some emergency surgery. This fascinates Steven – " Dr Elliott is taking a bleedy bit of jip out of the man's belly". Its helped enormously with blood tests, although he worries the doctor might drop an M&M into the cavity (Mr Bean in America). With language and familiarity, his fears have been lessened.

So, on to Friday:

Me – "Steve. Going to see doctor on Friday for blood needle".

Steven – " Steven's seeing Dr?....."

Me – "Guess. It's a doctor you haven't seen for a long time".

Steven – " Dr Hansen? Dr Hansen's going back to Holby City at Easter". (He is)

Me – "No. Not Dr Hansen. Steven's going to see Dr Vaughn Smith".

Steven – " Dr Vaughn Smith? With his moustache?"

Me – "What you going to say to Dr Vaughn Smith?"

Steven – "How's your moustache Dr Vaughn Smith?"

Me – "That'll be nice. And are you going to tell him how you are?"

Steven – "Steven Neary is fine Dr Vaughn Smith. Jip is all better".

Sorted. All I've got to remember to do now is to buy a bag of Maltesers. They worked as a blood test bribe in 2002 and the routine has stuck.

Living Room

I thought I'd start the New Year with an untypical cheery post – the story of Steven through his living room wall.

Yesterday, I wrote the post about the awful FACS assessment and how I don't recognise Steven at all from the reams of paperwork it produced. What I'd love to do is to send them a photo of his living room wall and say – "Stick this on the front of your file – it tells you everything you need to know about him".

When we moved into Steven's new home in November, I was determined that the living room would be his room, in his house. Walk into the room and there is very little sign that I live there at all. All my stuff – my books, my DVDs are in my bedroom. And every time I go into the living room, I smile as the shelf units and the pictures on the walls, show that Steven lives there. He is living in his living room. He has a life that is lived.

There are six pictures/posters on the wall – all of them absolutely crucial to Steven. He chose them. From right to left they are:

Raj's Painting of the stream:

Raj is one of the new friends Steven has made this year. You may remember that he got banned from Virgin Active after a few dreadful women from the water aerobics class complained that he was too noisy. That was that and on Mondays he now comes to work with me at the Arts Centre. Steven and his support worker use the music room where they listen to a compilation tape and play guitar and piano, pausing at "half time" for a cherry bakewell and an orange juice. In the next room is an art class, run by Raj. They hit it off immediately and a few weeks back, Raj presented Steven with a painting he'd done for him. With perfect timing, it was the week before me moved. Whenever Steven looks at the painting, he talks about Raj, and Arthur and Stan, the new friends he has made at Southlands. Such a contrast to the bitter attitude of the aerobic ladies.

Coronation Street calendar:

Steven loves Coronation Street. One interesting thing about that show is that it seems to allow Steven to express an emotional reaction that he is comfortable with. Feeling sad and crying usually throws him and can lead to a meltdown. The other week, he cried when Roy Cropper cried over the news that Hayley

14

was dying and he was able to keep it in perspective. Steven was sad because Roy was sad. Coronation Street also feeds Steven's love of impersonations and lookalikes. Not only does he think I look like Fred Elliott but I can do an impression of him as well. Whenever Steven meets someone new, he will do a Coronation Street lookalike thing with them – Raj at Southlands looks like Dev; Stan looks like Jack Duckworth and Arthur looks like Percy Sugden. These things play an important part in his communication and interaction with others.

Certificate from the gym:

I'm not quite sure why this certificate is so important to Steven. It goes back to 2009 and was awarded by Adam, Steven's personal trainer at the time, after Steven broke his personal best on the rowing machine. Adam was great and always made a big deal when Steven had a successful breakthrough, so I guess the certificate represents pride for Steven. The gym was always more about the people there than the exercises for Steven and when Adam left, Steven started to lose interest. The gym changed hands and is now a much bigger affair and Steven started to find the crowds there quite unsettling. It's a shame but the certificate represents a golden period when we saw the real benefits of people taking a genuine interest in Steven and how he responded.

Family Photos:

Beneath the certificate is a frame with about 12 family photos in. All his favourite people are there but interestingly, pictures of people that Steven never met – my mum and dad for example. With the photos, Steven loves to build up an extensive collection of back stories. There's a picture of me and my sister in the paddling pool as kids. Steven wanted to know all about the neighbours, what song was playing whilst we were in the pool (Blockbuster by The Sweet), what crisps we ate after we got out of the pool (blue Golden Wonder crisps), where Nanny Beryl and Granddad John were at the time (Beryl was making cheese on toast and John was having a shit) and he'll round off the story by announcing that, although the picture is probably 1973 and he wasn't born until 1990, he was in his mummy's belly at the time. Family are really important to Steven and this collage of photos provide an important narrative to his history, present and future.

Abba World:

We took Steven to Abba World, the exhibition of all things Abba for his 20th birthday, the year Steven was in the Unit. It was touch and go whether we'd get there because the Unit felt it was too much of a "risk" for him to go. This was a few weeks before the first DoL and in hindsight, I know that they had already started making plans. We thought we'd have to kidnap him to get him to the exhibition. Once there, he had a ball and the photo on the wall is a snap of Steven and me singing along to Dancing Queen. It was a great day – we rode in the helicopter from the cover of the Arrival album and appeared on stage with the Abba puppets. People who don't know Steven well get confused when he throws in the odd Sweden reference. Whenever we pass a reservoir or a small lake, Steven gets excited that he's seeing an archipelago. He will talk to complete strangers about Michael Tretow (Abba's sound engineer) or Uwe Magstroem (their costume designer). Abba are a good "let's try and distract from this meltdown" tactic. A quick enquiry into what colour jacket Bjorn is wearing in Fernando, normally stops a meltdown in its tracks.

Whistler's Mother:

Pride of place goes to the print of Whistler's Mother. Visitors get a bit thrown by this work of art amongst all the popular culture in the room but everything falls into place when Steven tells them what happened when Mr Bean went to America. Mr Bean saves the day on so many occasions. First thing in the mornings used to be a tricky time for Steven – all that unfilled space of the day lying ahead. Now, we start each day in the same fashion: bath, fruit and then a DVD/video. Monday is Top of the Pops; Tuesday is Men Behaving Badly, Wednesday and Saturday is Mr Bean; Thursday is Gladiators; Friday is Fawlty Towers and Sunday is Coronation Street. They start the day in a settled mood. Steven has an encyclopaedic knowledge of Mr Bean and is never happier than when he's recounting one of his adventures. As usual, every story must have a backstory, so we know what sandwich filling Angus Deayton had in the park bench scene, why Robin Driscoll had suddenly become blind at the bus stop scene and who was driving the army tank when Mr Bean's car got flattened. Of course, there was once the time when Mr Bean nearly cost Steven his liberty. I've written about it before but the Unit were compiling their evidence to send Steven to the hospital in Wales and they had put together a whole page of "incidents of concern" where Steven had been throwing things like jars of coffee, bottles of sauce and a tub of marmite, onto the floor. I tried to explain that Steven was acting out Mr Bean and pointed them in the direction of the episode where Bean redecorates his flat and drops all the above items on the floor but they wouldn't have it and these "acts of aggression" remained on file as evidence of his challenging behaviour. And it still satisfies me that Steven's lookalike for the social worker from 2010 is……. Whistler's Mother.

There are other things in the room that mark it out as Steven's space – his Basil Fawlty mask, his proud collection of Take That and Beautiful South CDs, his Gladiator annuals with the cover of Jet, who makes him go a bit soppy and red, on display. The latest addition to the living room is a set of Abba coasters that my sister got him for Christmas –

"Dad – it's a?........."

"They're Abba coasters Steve. Place mats"

"Dad – a coaster is a?......."

"A coaster is for putting things on"

"Putting things on........"

And with that, the Abba coasters now have a remote control placed on each of them.

This post may not be a FACS assessment. But I think it's a good snapshot of who Steven is, what floats his boat and what makes his life worth living.

Blowers

May 19, 2016

Paragraph from a report on mine and Steven's relationship, written by the Positive Behaviour Team during Steven's detention in 2010:

"Mr Neary refuses to acknowledge that by engaging in conversations with Steven that are strictly on Steven's terms, he is preventing Steven developing in more mature and appropriate ways".

Last night, I was sitting on the back door step, eating a cheeky Aero and Steven came bounding out:

" Dad – Henry Blowers, Dad".

"Henry Blowers mate?"

"Dad – Henry Blowers didn't sing Wake Me Up Before You Go Go".

" No mate. That was Wham".

Steven burst out laughing at his own joke and went skipping back into the living room like Michael Flately on speed.

I heard him chuckling and talking to himself:

"Steven Neary & Mark Neary was talking Henry Blowers. Massive funny George Michael joke. Steven Neary is a happy Cowley man".

Shirley Bassey & A Fancy

December 22, 2013

You may want to learn this off by heart. Just in case you happen to be in Cowley over the next three days and bump into a large autistic man who wants to engage you in conversation about his plans for the festivities. I've had to learn it and so have all the support workers, so I don't see why you should get off lightly......

"Sunday – Uncle Wayne and Auntie Jayne are popping in with Christmas presents.
At night time, watch Christmas Top of the Pops with Wizzard and Chip Richard

Monday – Mark Neary's going to get the Christmas potatoes.
Have a nice fancy at Southlands
Watch Toy Story 1 – To infinity and beyond

Tuesday – Go for a massive swim with Alan & Chris
Alan and Chris are going home early when Mark Neary is cooking the turkey
Watch Toy Story 2 with Big Al dropping his Wotsits on the floor. Get a bowl Al, you messy man"
Mark Neary will put the Christmas crisps and chocolates on the kitchen side bit by the Frosties"
Julie Neary will come for her sleep over.
Go to sleep and rest myself so I'm all fitter for Christmas Day"

Wednesday – Alan's got a day off – Mark Neary's doing my bath.
Open Christmas presents of a Mr Bean surprise, A Men Behaving Badly DVD, A Shirley Bassey CD & DVD, A massive Abba Surprise. And 28 more surprises.
Watch our new DVDs and listen to our new CDs.
After lunch, we can eat our Christmas Cheeselets and Christmas Maltesers and sing Goldfinger."

And as the pre big day anxiety cranks up, we're probably repeating that script (penned entirely by Steven) over 50 times a day.

June 13, 2015

We're home. And here is the set of postcards from the week in Torquay:

Sunday:

Here we are in Basil & Sybil territory. This is the view that greeted me over an al-fresco breakfast this morning. The sea does something to me emotionally. Well, any significant expanse of water does actually. I get the same reaction watching the barges along the canal. It's the completely different energy to the tempo of a town. So, eating my croissants, I am both in seventh heaven and tearful. Every holiday reminds me that, all things being unequal, instead of driving over to Babbacombe this afternoon, I could be on a train bound for a one hour visiting appointment with Steven in a Unit in Wales.

Life for learning disabled people is really that precarious. If things hadn't gone our way in 2011, we wouldn't have just shared an hour in the pool singing Here Comes The Summer. The fragility of a professional decision leaves me in a constant state of anxiety. Torquay today – what and where will next year bring?

But hey, I'm on holiday. Or rather I inhabit Steven's world of Fawlty Towers coming to life. A yacht sailed past earlier and Steven was convinced it was Mr Johnson at the helm ("Pretentious. Moi?") Last night, we spent a few hours in our own private pub and when I asked Steven what he wanted, he asked for, " a gin and orange, a lemon squash and a scotch and water please". He refuses to have kippers for breakfast, in case it brings about his demise like Mr Lemon. And when he saw his ensuite bathroom, he sneered rather ungraciously, "not big enough to drown a mouse". It's huge! But that doesn't fit with the Mrs Richards script.

The cottage is glorious and so is the generosity of the support workers. Yesterday, everyone pitched in. They assigned me one of the lower terrace bedrooms, so there are two floors between me and Steven, therefore ensuring an uninterrupted night's sleep. They took it in turns to dance the night away with Steven in the pub last night as he got sweatily excited over the wide choice of music on the jukebox.

I know how Shirley Valentine felt. Would anyone mind if we never came home?

Monday:

We've just got back from a morning at Shoalstone Pool in Brixham. There was a sign on the car park announcing that the pool was closed today for cleaning. Having travelled all the way from Cowley for a freezing, saltwater experience, I thought we can't turn back now, so descended the steps to the pool. There wasn't a soul there – no staff, no swimmers, so taking our bathing caps in hand we decided to brave it and if anyone noticed us, we'd pretend we hadn't seen the closure notice.

It's been two hours since we got out of the pool and I'm still shivering. Although I announced there would be a prize for the first person to fully submerge themselves, only Steven, me and two of the support workers had the balls. Funnily enough, within 30 seconds of entering the water our balls disappeared and haven't reappeared since. Steven gets confused by this – "Dad, Steven Neary's willy isn't there anymore". Disconcerting but we save the day by a quick burst of one of Take That's lesser known hits – " Scrotums ain't here anymore".

Somewhere in time, Steven became a lot more fearful about things. I've got photos of us at the same pool when Steven was seven. He was bombing down the ramp and just launched himself into the icy jellyfished water. Today, he got all anxious by the steps down to the pool and then spent about 10 minutes, up to his knees, reassuring himself – "It's alright Steven. Water will be hot in a minute". It does feel like this anxiety started after 2010, which I guess is not surprising as he spent a whole year living in fear.

I find it quite sad though that some former pleasures have disappeared off his agenda. He's already said he doesn't want to do the theme park tomorrow, whereas prior to 2010, a ride on the log flume would be one of his annual highlights. I remember coming down the flume at Blackpool pleasure beach in 2009 with him singing " The Time Warp "as we catapulted off the final drop. Carefree.

So this afternoon we're sticking to a normal Monday routine. He's listening to a Take That compilation tape at the moment and is planning a Mr Bean DVD straight after. He has allowed one concession to breaking the routine – we can have a barbecue tonight instead of spaghetti hoops.

And whilst Steven is enjoying Mr Bean in America, I'm going to jump into the fridge to warm up.

Tuesday:

This morning we went to the Splashdown Water Park. We had planned to go on a ferry ride from Torquay to Brixham. But showing unusual foresight, I phoned the ferry company earlier to find the sea was too choppy and all trips had been cancelled for the day. Thinking that perhaps we pushed our luck yesterday by swimming in a pool that was closed, it didn't feel quite the done thing to purloin a boat and take to the seas on our own. Breaking and entering is one thing – pirates is quite another.

It was another memory lane trip as we took Steven to the Water Park back in 1998. He remembered Julie paying the price for her brazenness when the waterfall sent her glasses spinning off her face.

I am fascinated by how the team building concordat is evolving. It is both hilarious and infuriating at the same time. Predictably, everyone is behaving completely predictably.

Last night in the pub, we had the team building darts competition. I was knocked out in the first round. I wouldn't say I was crap but I might have been more successful if I'd stood and held the dart and they threw the board at me. Steven took everyone by surprise by scoring a double 20 with his first throw. It was downhill all the way from that point, and like me, he had an early exit.

And now for a quiet afternoon watching The Full Monty. But we'll leave our sunhats on.

Wednesday:

After the hectic excursions of yesterday, we're having a quiet day in the cottage today. Wednesday is a fairly quiet day at home, so we are replicating it here. Mr Bean in America, A 90 minute disco, trip in minibus to Sainsburys for Munchies and a swim and spa planned for later.

Yesterday, one of the support workers suggested we hold a team meeting, giving me a chance to "express concerns" and vice versa. I wasn't keen. We used to have monthly team meetings when they were employed by the agency. The agency manager was pretty confrontational and most meetings ended up with a ruck between the workers. I didn't want to spoil the great atmosphere of the holiday and I don't have any collective concerns, so I suggested after Steven went to bed, we all stay up late and watch Field of Dreams together.

After the film, we shared stories of "if you build it, he will come" and "go the distance". It was revealing and moving. I won't share any of the support workers' stories here but I'll share mine. That film changes for me the older I get. I do believe that if something is important to us and we go the distance, anything is possible. When I was 16, my dream was to go to university and study journalism. Then my Mum died and I felt that my place was at home. I never went to university. I never became a journalist. But nearly 40 years later, after the desperate events of 2010, I have been able to become a writer. To me, that is the equivalent of Kevin Costner having a catch with his dead father.

Steven and I have just watched the psychiatrist episode of Fawlty Towers. It is our equivalent of playing catch. He likes to act out the scenes that have two male characters interacting. Telepathically, we divvy out the parts. He becomes Major and I'm Basil. When I'm dead and gone, I'd like Steven to regret that we can't have those moments anymore rather than we've never had those moments.

Steven has a new nickname today. One of the support workers who was around during the time in the ATU, reminded everyone of Steven's nighttime escape without footwear and in pyjamas. Prompted by last night's movie, today he called Steven, " Shoeless Steve".

Is this heaven?

Thursday:

Doesn't look like we're going to get our boat trip. For the third day running, the water was deemed too choppy and the ferry's remained in the harbour.

So we went on a steam train ride instead. Unable to find a Fawlty Towers reference for the trip, Steven dug deep into his memory bank and started singing, "Time flies by when you're the driver of a train. You can ride on the footplate, there and back again". Steven cast himself as Lord Bellborough and I became Mr Bracket, the butler. Yes – we're in Chigley. The support workers were, in order of appearance: Mr Rumpling, Mr Cresswell from the biscuit factory, Harry Farthing, Mr Swallow the wharf manager and Mr Antonio the ice cream man.

Back at the cottage, Mr Rumpling cooked a massive fry up to fortify ourselves for this afternoon's swim. The hot tub beckons, which will be lovely but we may need to wear woolly balaclavas for that part of us not submerged.

I've been reading another Community Care article which worries about the lack of paid RPRs for people subject to a DoL. Its another week, another DoLs piece bemoaning the excessive workload. It seems to me typical of Planet Social Care that it sets up something so bureaucratic and complicated and then complains about its own system. All very inward looking with little recognition of the people its meant to be serving. But then again, DoLs have become a huge industry.

So where have DoLs figured on our landscape this week? I think you'd need a high powered telescope to see a DoLs speck on the Torquay horizon. Family life and holidays are lived and conducted by ordinary people, outside of the industry. Therefore, the things that the industry consider of vital importance don't figure on a family's radar. We did a rudimentary risk assessment on the day of arrival and removed all ornaments and bric-a-brac. But that was it. We certainly haven't considered if Steven is being deprived of his liberty by having two people go with him to the swimming pool. Although they're called support workers, we don't use the word "supporting". The phrase "personal care" isn't in Steven's vocabulary – it's, "Dad – who's doing bath tonight?" That's how it should be. None of the industry self importance.

I'll sign off now. Steven, me and Mr Cresswell are going to have a game of table tennis in the pub. It's not in mint condition but it can certainly be used in an emergency.

Friday:

Hip hip hooray. And boo hiss.

Boo hiss because it's the last full day of this glorious holiday. Ever since I went to Pontins at 8, I've always been very melancholy on the last day of a holiday. As much as I want to enjoy the last few hours, a gloom descends. Steven, on the other hand, takes a last day very much in his stride and is already planning what he's doing when we get home tomorrow. In case you're interested that plan involves Toy Story 2 and a packet of Rolos.

We got up early today for a swim and a final dip in the spa pool before the maintenance men come to empty it. Steven is still very excited after our discovery yesterday afternoon. Driving back on the minibus, we passed an imposing white walled hotel with black piping. It even had a grassy slope outside. A couple emerged from inside the building and Steven immediately announced it was Mr & Mrs Hamilton from the Waldorf salad episode. The reality and the fiction finally meet on our penultimate day.

Hip hip hooray because we finally got our ferry ride. I was nervous on two counts. Firstly, I get seasick on a lilo. But more apprehensive because Steven has found a song for every moment of the holiday and the only boat song I thought he knew was The Lonely Island's " I'm on a motherf**king boat". Thankfully he remembered the 70s disco classic, Rock The Boat, so we were spared the disapproval of our fellow travellers.

It's been a fabulous week. So much better to be in a holiday cottage in Torquay than a hospital in Wales. I like to believe that Steven has a very good quality of life and having him around certainly improves the quality of my life. And we're so lucky to have the five great guys who came with us this week. One of them has taken over 100 photos that I'll post when we get home. They've all had a great time as well and I'm pleased that we've all been able to share this week.

And thank you Basil, Sybil, Manuel and Polly for providing our compass point all week.

When I started investigating my family tree last week, I was doing it purely for me and trying to solve some of the family mysteries that have rattled away in my brain for years. I hadn't considered the impact it would have on Steven. To say he's even more excited than me is the understatement of the year.

Steven is interested in people. He also loves stories. Put the two together, especially when it involves people he knows and he can find a hook, and he is in seventh heaven.

By Sunday morning, I'd reached the family layer of my great grandparents. The tree template allows you to upload photos of the people you discover. I don't have many photos from my parent's generation – the two main photos I have are the group photo from my wedding and the same from my parent's wedding. I enlisted the help of the support worker to take zoom shots of the many heads from these photos and once uploaded, I did crop jobs so they would all fit into the profile picture spaces. I like the end result, although the randomness of the photos plays havoc with the visual timeline. For example, the photo I have of my cousin was taken when she went to collect her MBE. She was in her early 60s. Yet the photo of her dad, my Uncle Albert, was taken during the war and he is probably in his late 20s.

Come Sunday evening and Steven wanted to see what I'd been up to. He was instantly hooked. Each photo and story eliciting yelps of excitement. It's always fascinating watching Steven store stuff on his internal hard drive. He has a look of intense concentration and the odd jerky head movement, which I take to be him filing the information in its rightful place. The look is the same when he's trying to retrieve something from the hard drive. The 8th hit of The Pet Shop Boys is readily retrievable but locating the name of the keyboard player from Martha & The Muffins may bring about a few jerks. At one point during the narration, Steven put his hand over my mouth. I guess I was going too fast for his download programme.

Steven only needs to be told something once and it is set in stone, to be remembered forever. An hour of telling family stories on Sunday night and he'll never forget them. Not being able to read or write, verbal stories are Steven's preferred (only?) mechanism to be part of an historical story. His inner library is vast. The Bodleian stored inside a blue sweatshirt.

Each night since Sunday, I've heard Steven rabbeting away to himself in bed for hours. "Mark Neary's dad is called Granddad John. Granddad John worked with big dogs. Granddad John's brother's name was Stanley. Uncle Stanley went on an aeroplane to Australia and never came back to Southall". I told him that story just the once. Similarly, " Mark Neary's mummy was Nanny Beryl. Nanny Beryl's brother was called Uncle Charlie. Uncle Charlie had a bacon and sausage shop in Southall. Then a new man came to the shop and Uncle Charlie drove massive lorries". Although it may sound, and may transpire, that after one hearing, Steven will just tell these stories by rote, I can tell they have done something to him. Whether it's about belonging, whether it's about connection, I'm not so sure. Maybe it's because they just strike him as dead good yarns.

In the final episode of Roots, Alex Haley went back to the village of Kunta Kinte. Seven generations had passed. Whilst there, he met the local griot. A griot is a tribal, oral historian. After listening for hours, Haley was finally reunited, 200 years later, with his great great great grandfather. No written records. Simply the oral narrative of an elderly man.

That's how Steven does it. He's the griot of Cowley.

A New Saturday Joke

May 3, 2014

Every day, after Steven has had his bath and his fruit salad, we spend time running through Steven's "busy day" ahead. Today's busy day started with three episodes of Chigley. During the run through Steven nearly had a meltdown caused because I'm not a mind reader, so didn't know what his unexpected plan was for just after tea.

"After lamb steak and carrots, Steven Neary is doing a massive joke. Steven Neary's doing different words".

Steven brought his plate into the kitchen after finishing his tea. His support worker was doing the washing up – I was cleaning the fridge.

"Are you ready Dad?" "Are you ready Michael?"

"I want my sun drenched, windswept, Ingrid Bergman kiss Not in the next life, I want it in Gary Linekar"

"Michael – time for bath".

Mr Bean & The Mental Capacity Assessment

October 1, 2012

Today was the day of the mental capacity assessment to determine if Steven has the capacity to manage the money he gets from the damages claim.

It was quite a palaver before we even got to the surgery. Steven's GP is on long-term sick and the other GP who knows him really well is on a month's holiday. It would probably have been very straightforward if either of them had been there. We ended up seeing a very nice GP who had never met Steven before. She wanted to see me first to get some background, so I arranged a ten minute appointment with her and then had to go back home to collect Steven and take him back for a second appointment 20 minutes later.

This is how the conversation went:

GP: Right Steven. Do you agree to your father managing your damages award?

Steven: (long pause) Watching Mr Bean this afternoon.

GP (even longer pause): Good. As I said, are you happy with that?

Steven: (no pause) Steven Neary's happy. Mr Bean's got a kettle stuck on his hand.

Assessment complete.

Goodnight John-Boy

July 17, 2013

Routine is vitally important for some people with autism. This is Steven's bedtime routine. It has grown considerably over the years and now takes about ten minutes every night. And if he forgets someone, or does the wrong order, he has to start from the beginning all over again:

"Goodnight Mrs Doubtfire
Goodnight Mark Neary
Goodnight Gary Barlow
Goodnight Rowan Atkinson
Goodnight John Clark (He's the guy who held the nurses hostage in Brookside in 1983)
Goodnight Fash
Goodnight Ulrika
Goodnight Trojan
Goodnight Jet – the beautiful Jet
Goodnight Sophie Ellis Bextor and Spiller
Goodnight Diego (our nest door neighbour)
Goodnight Jodie Keary (his cousin)
Goodnight two Granddads
Goodnight Manuel & The Major *
Goodnight Zippy & Bungle *
Goodnight Fred Elliot *
Goodnight Rolf Harris *
Goodnight Anthony, Brian, John and Terry (East 17)
Goodnight Busman John with his keys (his old school transport driver)
Goodnight Dave Hemmingway (The Beautiful South)
Goodnight Alan & John (The Rubettes – followed by a chorus of Sugar Baby Love)
Goodnight Bill Hislop (Muriel's Wedding)
Goodnight Mark Neary"

The one's I've marked with *, I'm expected to join in with because I can do impressions of those.

I've been clearing the flat out in preparation for the move and last night I came across the box with all the court papers and witness statements in them. Stupidly, I started to re-read some of them.

This from the positive behaviour unit:

"Mr Neary met with (Managers from the unit) to share his views on how to support Steven when he becomes anxious. Some of the points he raised were very useful. However, the ritualistic and repetitive nature of some of his responses are not considered to be productive or helpful in moving Steven forward and change his inappropriate behaviours"

The bedtime routine was the one I had quoted as an example.

Sleep.

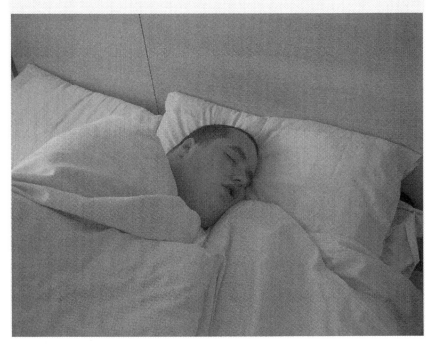

Professional to Steven: "Have you been out on your community programme this morning Steven?"

Steven: "No. Steven Neary's been swimming".

I love Steven's direct way with language. I love his whole relationship with language. Most of all, I love the way he cuts through all the bullshit and goes straight to the heart of the matter. I get envious and wish I could be more like him.

If Steven isn't understanding what the other person is saying, he has three stock phrases:

"Lady's doing silly talking".

"Why don't you talk properly" (Thank you Basil Fawlty)

"Man's doing MFL talking. Like Steven Neary in class 6 with David Watson"

For the uninitiated, MFL is Modern Foreign Languages. That lesson was a constant source of excitement but bewilderment for Steven. He'd go into the sweet shop and say, "Bonjour Ranjit. A Caramac s'il vous please". On Wednesdays. On Sundays however, he'd revert to English, leaving Ranjit totally perplexed. MFL class was on Wednesdays, so I'd like to think that Steven believed that you only use "different words" on Wednesdays.

Perversely, being an Abba fan, he has never for one moment questioned that Swedish might be a MFL. After getting an Abba documentary DVD, Steven plagued me to buy their music pre and post Abba. So, I'd be searching through Amazon Sweden for CDs by The Hootenanny Singers and The Hep Stars. Post Abba, Anna Frid released an album and the lead track was "Aven en Blooma". It's sung entirely in Swedish but Steven knows all the words. He doesn't acknowledge that she is singing in another language. To make it more surreal, Steven sings it in his London accent so it comes out as "Having a bloomer". Like a cross between Dizzee Rascal and Dick Van Dyke via a Stockholm archipelago.

He doesn't like change in words. I got him the deluxe copy of Take That's "Beautiful World". The non-deluxe copy was turned deluxe by adding a DVD of three hits and two extra tracks. Also, the deluxe version of Rule the World has an extra verse. Every time he listens to it, he says: "Dad – different words Dad. Gary Barlow – what do you think you're doing?"

Yesterday, I watched a Southern Health video, where KP was trying to inspire her staff by telling them they are inspiring.

I wonder what Steven would make of it if he was sitting in the audience:

"Dad. Lady's doing silly talking. You can't push an envelope Lady. You can push a trolley in Tesco but you can't push an envelope".

"Dad. Lady's a vanguard Dad. Bit like the Fat Controller".

"Dad. Lady's got the shivers with the inspirations. Better put a cardigan on Lady".

Or he might have just eaten all the cakes.

Better still. Sod KP. Sod the cakes. Have a bloomer with Anna Frid instead:

Back To The Flood
February 26, 2017

Watching Robbie appear with Take That again last night and singing The Flood took both Steven and me back to that night in 2010 when Steven escaped from the ATU whilst Take That were reuniting on the X Factor and singing The Flood live for the first time.

"Do you remember Steve?"

"Steven Neary ran away from M House with his pyjamas on".

"Steve was a very brave young man. You didn't put your shoes and socks on".

"Steven Neary had massive sore feet. Steven Neary was very brave".

And then a few seconds later, thankfully, he can turn that horrible event into a joke:

"Steven Neary's not going to run away from the Cowley house when Take That sing don't go holding back the flood. Cowley house is the best house".

Which is a very nice perspective.

And in case you're wondering, Jason Orange wasn't singing with Take That last night because according to Steven, "Jason Orange is still looking at the sharks in Australia".

Politeness

In a blink of an eye, Steven has discovered a new expression that to the unknowledgeable listener may suggest that Steven has spent the last few years in a finishing school. Manners have become the new currency.

It was only a couple of weeks ago that me and the support workers were chuckling over Steven's complete absence of regard for the other. I'm alright Jack was our coat of arms.

Two examples. One of my new pairs of training bottoms went missing. We searched everywhere for them. Eventually the support worker found them in a crumpled heap at the bottom of Steven's wardrobe. I asked Steven how they came to be there and he replied, "Steven Neary put them in the wardrobe". When I asked him why, his explanation was "Trousers was on Steven Neary's radiator". Straightforward. They were on his radiator. They weren't his. He has no use for them. Get rid.

Des, the support worker told me a similar story. He (Des) was in the kitchen preparing his own meal. A dish of chicken and rice, he had ingredients all over the worktop. Steven came into the kitchen and said he wanted his sausage and spaghetti hoops. As Steven can cook them himself, Des left him to it. When he returned to the kitchen, all his food had disappeared. He asked Steven what had happened to his tea and got the reply, "In the bin". Again, straightforward. Chicken and rice had no place with sausage and spaghetti hoops so had to go.

Overnight, we now have a new phrase – "If you want to". On Sunday, we were doing a compilation tape and I asked Steven what song he wanted next. "Dad. Have some Gene Pitney. If you want to". This morning, Steven wanted a private chat, away from the support workers – "Dad. Can you come in the kitchen? If you want to". He was asking who is going to be working on Christmas Day & when I told him, he said to the support worker – "Francis, you can have white turkey on Christmas Day. If you want to".

I don't think Steven has suddenly mastered unconditional positive regard. More likely, is he heard Dr Hanssen say it on Holby City. It's a totally unexpected development.

I've tried to be more like Steven and be more direct in my communication. I've been trying not to let my awkwardness over certain social conventions render me speechless. Today, I blew it. The gym I've started going to is run by the former Gladiator, Panther. It's called Panthers. I keep wanting to ask her if I can bring Steven along one day to meet her. Panther isn't Jet but Steven would still see it as a big feather in his cap. I see her there often but she's normally in the middle of a workout and I think it's terribly bad form to interrupt someone on the treadmill. This afternoon, she was on the front desk and I thought "Carpe Diem". As I approached, her phone went off and for me, the moment had passed. It felt uncomfortable mooching around whilst she took the call, so I went on in and started my session.

If it had been Steven, it would have been very different:

"Hello Panther. Talk to Steven Neary. If you want to".

Steven Neary & Boy George

August 19, 2013

Steven is fascinated by the relationship between Boy George and Jon Moss, the Culture Club drummer. Steven is always keen to build up an extensive back story to a picture, song lyric or video clip. In the narrative of this Culture Club relationship, Steven has built up George as a demanding figure, expecting Jon to pander to his every whim (which may not be too far from the truth).

This all began after Steven watched the DVD of the Culture Club 25th anniversary concert. During the encore of "Bow Down Mister", George looks across to Jon, and says: "Bring it down Jonny boy". For some reason, Steven finds this line hysterically funny – even after 100 viewings. I've tried to explain what George meant but that only compounds his mirth. Wiping away tears of laughter, Steven says: "Don't be silly Dad – Drums are noisy – can't have quiet drums".

I have a vinyl copy of George's solo single, "Sold". On the sleeve, George has blood on his neck. True to form, Steven invented a whole story for the picture, whereby George had cut his neck on some very sharp violin strings. And the dialogue in Steven's story is: "Plaster please, Jonny boy".

I found a copy of the 1983 Culture Club Annual in a charity shop. In it, there is a photo of a gentrified looking Boy George sipping a cup of tea, probably sending up his famous quote. Not only does Steven flesh out this photo with a full list of the foods that were served at this feast, but he casts Jon in the subservient role again with the line: "Milk and two sugars please Jonny boy".

Last night we watched the video of "Do You Really Want To Hurt Me". In one scene, George emerges from a swimming pool, fully clothed. After much tut tutting, Steven ordered: "Trunks please, Jonny boy".

I love these stories and Steven's imagination. They bring a tiny ache as well as they highlight the two Stevens: the one that he really is and that everyone knows, and the Hillingdon version. In the many lever arch files I have of professional reports, these sort of stories never get a mention and yet they contain everything you need to know about Steven's thinking, his humour, his communication – basically his world view.

Never mind – it's their loss. "Valuing people, Jonny boy".

I remember watching Peter Ustinov being interviewed by Parkinson many years ago. They were discussing dinner parties and those people who pin you to the wall to get you to agree with their opinion. Ustinov claimed to have found the perfect response/exit line. You wait until the person leans back, confident they have delivered their killer shot and say:

"Ah yes. Very good point. But not in the South".

They will be so bemused by this, you can slip away whilst they are still working out whether they heard correctly.

Steven has a similar approach to a debate. Just when you think you have all bases covered, he will deliver a perfect Ustinov googly.

This morning, Steven was having a music session with Chris, his support worker. The track "My Camera Never Lies" came on.

Chris: "Steve – do you think that Bucks Fizz are a bit like Abba?"

Steven: "No. Chris is talking like a silly man. Bucks Fizz is not like Abba. No beards in Bucks Fizz".

Chris, knowing that Steven likes lookalikes/sound-alikes decides to pursue the theme:

Chris: "So, are Boney M a bit like Abba?"

That was just met with total derision.

Steven: "TUT. Boney M is not like Abba. Boney M sounds a bit like Ottawon".

I decide to chip in with perhaps Steps are a bit like Abba. Steven concedes that the video to Last Thing On My Mind is a bit Abbaesque but dismisses my reasoning because there are "three ladies in Steps".

Chris throws in another couple of suggestions but they are given short shrift. Eventually, he tries to return serve:

Chris: "So, who is a bit like Abba then Steve?"

Steven: "Ace of Base is a bit like Abba"

Fair play to Chris – he has seen the All That She Wants video and thinks he is on a winner:

Chris: "But the men in Ace of Base haven't got beards Steve?"

Steven, with the withering look of a man who can't quite believe someone would put forward such a facile argument, pulls out his trump:

Steven: "Ace of Base is a bit like Abba because Ace of Base live near the archipelago. Like Bjorn Uvelus writing Fernando".

Chris knows he is beaten and sidles off to the kitchen for a restorative biscuit. He knows he has been Ustinoved.

Steven is never smug in his victories. By now, the CD has moved on to "It Ain't What You Do It's The Way That You Do It". And Alan, the second support worker for swimming, has walked through the door.

Steven: "Chris – Siobhan looks like Auntie Jayne with her blue shirt and purple leggings on. And Neville looks a bit like you Alan".

Chris takes refuge in the saucepan cupboard.

Musical Chairs
April 23, 2013

Good news. I've finally ordered Steven his new sofa.

I picked up a catalogue from our local store (I didn't want to run the risk of Steven trying out several sofas for size in-store) and brought it home to show Steven.

The sofas have all got female names: Chloe, Marigold, Bronwyn, Fenella. Normal names but carrying a slightly saucy ring when applied to a sofa.

After three minutes of browsing, guess which one Steven plumped for?........ A Lola.

Nothing to do with the smooth upholstery; the firm springs; the delightful selection of colours.

No, he chose a Lola, so we can sing: "Her name was Lola. She was a showgirl......"

Have I set myself up for years of agony, where every time someone sits down on the sofa, Steven gets them to sing a quick chorus of Barry Manilow?

"Life in The Neary Household – The Musical", will shortly be coming to a theatre near you.

Two Dead Pigeons

May 28, 2016

Yesterday, I was in Northampton for the second consecutive Friday. Last week I was invited to tell the Get Steven Home story to a group of social workers and clinical staff at St Andrews. Yesterday, I was back on familiar territory as my favourite MCA trainer, Wendy Silberman, had booked me again to speak to her latest cohort of BIAs.

During the afternoon session, we got into a discussion about the amount of time a BIA has to carry out a best interests assessment. It seemed like the going rate was between 2 to 3 hours. I was asked what I felt about that.

It doesn't seem very long at all to me. I appreciate that since Cheshire West the demand to turn around DoLs applications is enormous but I can't see possibly how the fullest and fairest assessment can be conducted in 3 hours. I said that it takes people ages to tune into Steven's unique way of speaking and without that tuning, valuable information is likely to pass them by. I told them about Steven's Mental Capacity assessment to see if he had the capacity to manage a tenancy! When I got home, I asked him how it had gone. He very cheerfully announced, "Connie was doing Pet Shop Boys talking". After a while the penny dropped and realised that she had been talking about Tenants and Rent. For someone who had just met Steven, that would have gone right over their heads.

Today brought a great example. Steven came into the kitchen this morning as me and the support worker were having a conversation about the small wet patch that has appeared on the bathroom ceiling. The support worker said that there might be a problem with the water tank (which is in the loft).

Straightaway, Steven was on the job, "Michael – go up to the roof and take two dead pigeons out of the water tank".

A couple of minutes later he passed me the phone and said, "Dad – phone Mr Wilkins. Send right away for the plumber".

For those not in the know, Mr Wilkins was the plumber in Trumpton who came to install a new water tank in the Town Hall after the Mayor kept getting drips on his ceremonial hat.

This afternoon, the plumber arrived. He was a Sikh chap with a bright red turban.

"Hello Mr Wilkins. Nice to meet you", said Steven as he went to the door.

They had a brief chat about pigeons and then Mr Wilkins got on with his business.

I wonder how it would have gone if, instead of fitting a new ballcock, Mr Wilkins had come to do a best interests assessment.

A Search For Bono

December 7, 2014

Another question of grave importance has just arisen for Steven as he listens to U2 during his Sunday morning music session:

"Dad – Bono hasn't found what he's looking for. Bono's looking for his what Dad?"

"Dunno Steve. Perhaps Bono's looking for his socks?"

"Not socks Dad. Bono's socks are on Bono's feet".

" Don't know Steve. What is Bono looking for?"

" Bono's looking for his blue Walkers salt and vinegar square crisps".

"Has Bono found them Steve?"

"Bono's crisps are in Simon LeBon's belly. Bono is cross".

Dilemma sorted, Steven carries on with his session, occasionally muttering, " fucking Simon LeBon"

Deprived of Liberty In A Yellow Mini

Another day and another dreadful example of Steven being deprived of his liberty.

Today's DoL took place at the Motor Museum:

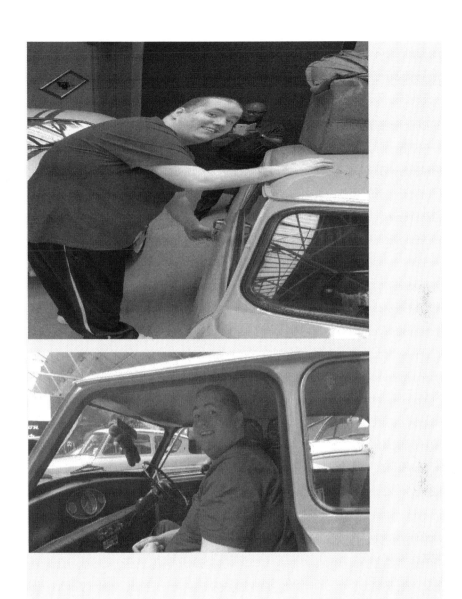

Two Christmas Play stories. I find them really distressing to write but they do end with a Steven, Monday joke.

Yesterday evening, Steven dug out an old video from his schooldays. This one was from 1997 (so, he would have been 7) and that Christmas, the school put on "Children's TV Favourites" for its Christmas Show. Steven's class did Bananas In Pyjamas and Steven was over the moon to get one of the main parts – B2. Steven was loving watching it back, giving a running commentary to his support worker on who all the main players were. I found it too upsetting to watch and slinked off to the kitchen and protected myself by cleaning the kitchen cupboards. What was so distressing for me was how the 17 years since have treated the class of 97. Over half of them are either dead, trapped in ATUs, stuck in so-called independent living flats, or in residential accommodation hundreds of miles from their families. All that innocent joy as a class of bananas sang their hearts out to "we're coming down the stairs" has been stolen by the stinking, dis-interested world of adult social care. Those kids deserved **SO** much better from the world.

On to today. Steven's history with Sting goes back to the 1999. That year the school put on "Millennium Here we Come" and Steven's class did the moon landing. They entered the stage to "Walking On The Moon", so Steven became interested in The Police. In the programme for the production, Steven is listed as "Neil Armstrong" but ask him and he said: "Steven Neary's playing Sting".

This morning Steven turned up at the Arts centre for his morning music session. Yesterday, we did a compilation tape for him to play back today. We have been working through the alphabet and have reached artists beginning with P (The Pet Shop Boys, Puff Daddy, Peters & Lee). The first track was "Every Breath You Take"

Steven: Dad – Sting's playing a ......?

Me: It's a double bass Steve.

Steven: A Bass! Like a pizza base.

46

He found this idea hysterically funny – "Sting. Don't get pepperoni on your double bass. You'll make your fingers all saucy"

Thank goodness he has got support workers who are as caring and interested as those staff in Bananas in Pyjamas. I know, that whilst I'm away later, if Steven starts to get anxious or worked up, one of them will say: "Steve – tell us your Monday joke about Sting" and everything will be all right.

We Are Golden

I'm feeling terribly nervous about the final episode of Endeavour next Sunday. All the clues are pointing to a fatal end for Fred Thursday. Last week ended with his soldier son saluting him and today's finished with Thursday laying his hand on Morse's shoulder as he left the pub.

I've never had a work relationship like Morse and Thursday. I can't imagine Steven ever saluting me and as he doesn't really like being touched, a hug or a hand is a rare event.

But then I thought about this afternoon. Steven was looking for one of his compilation DVDs – "The DVD with Mika with his pants on"

I found it and it prompted the following story from Steven:

"Mika! Don't dance about with just your pants on.

You might get a chill Mika.

What would Adam Lewis say to you Mika?

Adam would say – You won't get fitter if you've got a nasty chill.

Put some clothes on Mika and sort yourself out".

(For background, Adam Lewis is Steven's old personal trainer. Adam liked Mika's first big hit, Grace Kelly. Adam's mantra at the start of every session was "Let's get going Steven and get you fitter.")

I love Steven's flying imagination. I love how he can pull several threads of his life together to create a funny story. And he knows he is creating a funny narrative because he's smiling as he tells the story. I love how he takes it upon himself to give Mika the benefit of his wisdom.

He doesn't have those conversations with anyone else. I guess with me, he knows that I will know all the reference points and that enables his imagination to take flight.

These are our Thursday and Morse moments.

They're Golden.

The Paul Simon Years

As is my annual want over the August bank holiday weekend, I updated my list of my top 500 songs of all time. It is crucial, vanguard work. Who knows, over the past 12 months my affection for Altered Images' Don't Talk To Me About Love may have grown sufficiently to move it upwards from number 152 to number 133. It is important that that 19 place ascent is noticed and recorded.

Steven loves the chart rundown which we'll tape over the next few weeks. He doesn't like it if I put two songs by the same artist back to back like I did once with Teenage Rampage and The Six Teens by The Sweet at numbers 302 and 303.

The only song Steven and I disagree hugely on is Paul Simon's You Can Call Me Al. I have it at number 221. Steven would have it in the top five. It's a big song for Steven. He came across the video first and developed one of his detailed back stories for it. Chevvy Chase lip syncs the lyrics in the video which threw Steven. "Chevvy Chase has got Paul Simon's voice in his mouth". But what threw Steven more was where was Mr Garfunkel? In the end he decided that Art had gone to Woolworths to buy some new brown shoes and a Cadburys Flake.

Steven thinks it's very funny to play with the lyrics and when peoples' names appear in lyrics, he goes into overdrive. And in You Can Call Me Al, you've got two. Al and Betty. Al is the soldier in the army tank that runs over Mr Bean's car in Unseen Bean. And Betty is Betty Hislop, the mother of the bride in Muriel's Wedding. So, in the Cowley house, the chorus goes:

" I can call you Betty Hislop who died. You can call me Al who squashed Mr Bean's car ".

I'll let you into a secret. The first time Steven came across Simon and Garfunkel was seeing a clip of them at the famous Central Park gig. It was Bridge Over Troubled water where Paul has stormed off in a huff, leaving Art to sing on his own. Since that day, Steven has called him Simon Garfunkel, not Art, and nothing is going to change that now it's embedded on Steven's hard drive. " Dad. Simon and Simon. That's a bit greedy".

Two other Simon and Garfunkel songs that make it into Steven's top 100 are Mrs Robinson and Cecilia. When we sing these two, Steven changes the lyrics to:

"So here's to you Steven Robinson. Don't fall on the mat in Hang Tough". Steven Robinson was a contender in the 1993 series of Gladiators. And,

" Its Cecilia. From Mencap pool with her long finger nails" because Cecilia is Tom's gran at the Friday evening swim.

There you have it. A one page profile, solely on Steven's relationship with Paul Simon.

Whatever Happened to Bruce Foxton?

April 9, 2014

I wish I'd been in the car to swimming yesterday. We're in the second week of the new contract with the new cab company and I have to say, I'm really impressed. All the drivers are going out of their way to click with Steven. None more so than Mack, yesterday's driver.

Despite his love of music, Steven doesn't normally like music in a car and will ask the driver to turn the radio off. However, yesterday as he sat down, "Speak Like A Child" was playing.

"Mack – it was Style Council's first song of Speak Like A Child".

Mack, who obviously knows his stuff replied:

"You know Paul Weller then Steve?"

"Yes. The Jam are all gone. We've got the Style Council now".

They sang for a bit and then Mack said:

"So The Jam have all gone then Steve. I wonder whatever happened to Bruce Foxton?"

"Bruce Foxton's gone to a new work in a pub. And Rick Buckler's a lollipop man now".

Which may, of course, be true......

A Tiny Seed

I'm meant to get a lay in on a Sunday morning. I do go back to bed after the support worker arrives but the conversation from downstairs is so gripping, I find it impossible to go back to sleep. The plan is that the support worker does Steven's bath and breakfast. Then I run through the Sunday script with Steven, confirming the running order of the day and then return to bed. Steven then watches the introduction to Match Of The Day – he's not bothered about the football but he likes to know who's on the panel. Then, they listen to a C90 compilation tape that Steven and I prepared the afternoon before.

It is the interaction during the tape that is so distracting. Nick, the support worker, is the same age as Steven but he has very little musical knowledge prior to 1990 – his musical tastes only stretch to drum and bass. This is a genre Steven has never really got into – The Proclaimers not including much drum and bass in their back catalogue. This disparity in their musical experience is what makes their conversation so fascinating.

For those of you who may wish to act out the following vignettes at your next theatre workshop. I've included some performance notes to help with your characterisation:

Steven: Earnest, delighted to have someone interested in him but slightly bemused that he knows more than his carer. Nick: Eager to engage but keenly aware that he's having an intense learning experience.

This is how Sunday's conversation went:

Track One:
Nick: "Who is this Steve?"
Steven: "Wheatus – Teenage Dirtbag"
Nick – "When was this Steve?"
Steven: "When Steven Neary was in David Watson's class. Class 1. Steven Neary sang Wheatus in act of worship on Thursday afternoon".

Track Two:
Nick: "Who is this Steve?"
Steven: "Sparks – This Town Aint Big Enough"

Nick: "When was this Steve?"
Steven: "Long time. Massive long time"
Nick: "Where was Steven Neary?"
Steven: "Steven Neary was not here yet. Steven Neary was a tiny seed".

Track Three:
Nick: "Who is this Steve?"
Steven: "The Beautiful South – 36D"
Nick: "When was this Steve?"
Steven: "Steven Neary was in Scunthorpe. Steven Neary was eating four bourbon biscuits".
(The song continues)
Steven: "Nick – no ladies in 36D"
Nick: "No ladies in 36D?"
Steven: "Just the men. Brianna Corrigan's left. Jacqui Abbott's not here yet".
Nick: "So, just the men?"
Steven: "And Chook from Muriel's Wedding."

Track Four:
Nick: "I know this one Steve – It's Coolio"
Steven: "No. It's Coolio featuring LV".
Nick: "When was this Steve?"
Steven: "It was Steven Neary's first Christmas in Hillingdon. Steven Neary was in Maggie Tesei's class. Had Coolio and LV on Christmas Top of The Pops with Jack Dee and Bjork"
Nick: "Was Jack Dee the host?"
Steven: "Jack Dee was talking – and now for a marvellous musical montage starting with Coolio and LV"

And so it went on. Nick was taught about the sort of chocolates that Cilla Black eats (Ferrero Rocher); How Gary Barlow came to have jelly up his bum and why Benny Anderson won't shave his beard off.

Would you sleep?

Carry On Roofing

This week, after 6 months of pontifications from the housing association, we finally got the hole in the roof repaired. No more buckets in my bedroom. Steven chatted to Dan, one of the roofers, and was chuffed to learn that Dan was a Proclaimers fan.

Stevens only reference point for someone getting up on the roof is Jim Dale in Carry on Doctor. So when he saw Dan on top of the house, he yelled out:

"Dad! Come and look. It's a rooftop drama".

It reminded me of two other Carry on moments during medical appointments. There was the embarrassing time with the rather large dental assistant when Steven looked her straight in the eye and said: " Lady looks like Hattie ".

And the time with the paediatrician who didn't like Steven. At the end of an appointment, he asked Steven if he had any questions. Steven, who had been briefed that this man was a doctor like Dr Tinkle, thought about it and asked:

" Kenneth Williams is a funny man because.....?"

I've developed a bit of a pattern that does me no favours at all. Whenever I'm feeling a bit under the weather, I go into obsessive preparations for Steven's future when I'm no longer around. When I should just be resting, I hurl myself into frantic planning & activity.

I've had a few days of a throat infection with my voice disappearing as the day wears on. A casual remark by one of the support workers on Tuesday triggered a major project that has kept me occupied when I should have been resting up.

Each week, Steven has a rota of DVDs and videos that he watches. We will watch an episode of say, Fawlty Towers together and two days later, after breakfast, he will watch the same episode back by himself. The weekly rota is:

Monday (and Wednesday): Mr Bean

Tuesday (and Thursday): Gladiators

Wednesday (and Friday): Fawlty Towers

Thursday (and Saturday): Camberwick Green

Saturday (and Monday): Top of The Pops

Sunday (and Tuesday): Men Behaving Badly

You will notice we don't have a rota for Friday. That's because its my long day at work, so Steven will chose something that doesn't fit into any of the above categories. Anyway, on Tuesday, the support worker asked me if there was an order to the Men Behaving Badly viewing. There is but it's stored in mine and Steven's internal filing system. We don't watch the episodes in order of transmission. It's more random than that. The upshot was that I convinced myself I urgently needed to document these rotas.

Like most of Steven's routines, I decided to do a pictorial record, so he could take charge of it as well as the support staff. No problem at all with most of the programmes – Google images has plenty of Fawlty Towers stills. I even managed to get pictures of the 12 Top of the Pops episodes we watch on a loop (the Christmas episodes from 1995 to 2003 & a few TOTP2 specials).

Gladiators was the sticking point. Steven watches videos of two first round heats from 1993, the 1993 quarters and semi-finals and the grand final. He's also got the 1994 semi-finals and finals. I tried to get away with missing Gladiators out! No chance...

"Dad. No Gladiators pictures! Want a picture of Roddy McKay's shorts falling down in Hang Tough".

To cut a long story short, I did it. Took me two days. I'm no techie but I managed to get screen shots from YouTube of all 12 episodes. Even a shortsless Roddy McKay. Much to my pride, I even found that pants wettingly exciting moment from Heat 1 in 1993 when Nightshade knocked Pauline Oliver off suspension bridge with 1 second to go. I'm back in the good books again.

I'm going to make that support worker pay for activating my manic activity. If he doesn't know which contender cut his nose on Skytrack in the 2nd quarter final of 1993 Gladiators by Thursday, I'll be docking his pay. And if he doesn't learn that Paul Field & Eunice Huthart were the 1994 Champions, he'll be shown the door.

" Chris. You will be sacked on my first whistle. 3.2.1....."

Afternoon Tea With Coolio

March 5, 2013

I heard Steven chatting to his support worker whilst he was in the bath this morning – "Steven Neary's got a very busy hard work today".

And he was right. This was his gruelling day:

– Watched an episode from the 1993 quarter finals of Gladiators.

– Off to Virgin Active for his water aerobics and spa pool.

– Changed the sheets on his bed.

– Did a compilation music tape that he's been planning since the weekend. "Going to have Coolio and Bucks Fizz".

– Watched the Fawlty Towers episode with Mr O'Reilly, the builder. Running commentary throughout.

– Over an hour and half on the computer looking for clips of Moby.

– Catalogued the photos of his grandmother by dress colour.

Interestingly, he didn't include loading up the washing machine and doing the washing up as part of his hard work day.

As he got out of the cab after swimming, the driver asked Steven what he had planned for the afternoon:

"It's a big busy. Got Coolio. It's a marvellous musical montage".

One Glove & Pete Burns

Steven became totally institutionalized around bed times during the year he was in the ATU. He'd have his bath and be in his pyjamas by 6pm and then take himself off to bed at 9pm. The things he used to do when he was younger, going to a midweek match, or the monthly disco, disappeared off his radar. Try as we might to encourage him, they've never reappeared on the radar.

On Friday, he saw a trailer for the ITV special "The Greatest Number 1s of the 80s, which aired last night at 9pm. Right up Steven's street but a break from routine. He spent the whole day working out how to accommodate the programme. It was as detailed as a military manoeuvre.

" Dad – have my lovely packet of Chewits before all the good songs show?"

"Dad – do my goodnight wee when the adverts are on?"

"Dad – no goodnight talking later. Straight to sleep?"

Plan in place. Adam Ant, we're ready for you.

The support worker was in awe. There was no artist or group Steven didn't know. It was one of those talking heads sort of shows with the usual suspects (Pete Waterman, Stewart Copeland) and he knew all of them too. He occasionally got thrown by how different people looked in their old age ("Nick Kershaw's got a grey beard. He's an old man now"). Or looking different just because you're Pete Burns. ("No more patches. Pete Burns' eye is all better").

As the countdown to number one built, the excitement cranked up.

"Gordon Bennett. It's The Human League. Phil Oakey's washed his lipstick off", or

" Michael Jackson's just got one glove on. That's a bit silly Michael. Where's your two gloves? Michael Jackson dropped his glove at Windsor when he went to feed the swans".

As my mum used to say, "They're all in it". The Pet Shop Boys, Wham, Culture Club, all of them with their own Steven Neary back story. The support worker got a bit choked up in a combination of nostalgia and impressiveness at Steven's invention.

All in all, a nice break from the routine. Steven coped with his own change and we all got a lay in this morning. And it's supplied a soundtrack to today as well. Whilst having his bath this morning, I heard Steven say: " Francis. Good joke. Come on Eileen Grimshaw".

And just now: "When two tribes go to Ranjit's sweet shop".

All, so much nicer and normal than being packed off to bed at 9.

Mightiness & Maggots

I've been booked to give a talk tomorrow morning for one of the big care agencies in our neighbouring borough. It was arranged ages ago and I contacted them today to double check the arrangements. It was a good job I did. I assumed that they wanted me to do my Get Steven Home talk. They didn't. They heard that one two years ago. They want something more specific to their audience and have given me the title "What Makes A Good Support Worker".

Coincidentally, I've been collating the stories for Seven days of Action and one of the excuses that comes up time and again as to why people stay so long in ATUs is that they can't find appropriate, trained staff to support the home care package. I always feel my hackled being raised whenever I hear that excuse.

My job specification consists fundamentally of five "qualities":

1. Be interested in Steven.
2. Be authentic
3. Engage
4. Be funny
5. Be professional.

In that order. Steven doesn't need manual handling, so you don't need to go on a manual handling course. I can run Mental Capacity Act training for the support workers. In fact, we just had a very lively session on the five principles. And I don't need someone who can write a comprehensive risk assessment of the Mencap Pool or the gym.

One story that I will tell tomorrow to illustrate all of the above.

For Steven's recent birthday, I managed to get him the missing Gladiators VHS tape that he was missing from his collection. We have tapes with five of the eight first round heats from the 1993 series, the four quarter final episodes and the semi final and grand final. Amazon came up trumps with a VHS that contained heats 6 to 8 from the 1993 series.

Gladiators is Steven's "centering" viewing on a Thursday morning. Each day, Steven will watch an episode from a favourite TV show after his breakfast and it focuses him on the day ahead. We've learned over a number of years that if Steven has unfilled time first thing in the morning, he can get very agitated and a meltdown is never far away. So, Wednesdays is an episode of Mr Bean, Friday is Fawlty Towers etc. etc. Steven has had the same support worker on Thursday mornings for the past three years.

So there we were on birthday morning, Steven slips in the VHS and up pop contenders that we are familiar with from the later quarter final programmes. Michael, the support worker, immediately said:

"Hey Steven. Look who it is. It's Sirleen – the mighty maggot".

A huge grin spread over Steven's face. He got up and started doing his Tigger bounce around the living room. He was excited because the support worker had recognised the contender and in that recognition, Steven's and Michael's worlds met. It was beautiful and very moving.

Someone told me a long time ago that if you wait for someone with autism to enter your world, you'll be waiting a bloody long time. Best thing to do, if you want to connect, is to enter their world and then, you might engage.

For the past three years between 7am and 8am, the support worker hasn't been on his phone. He's not been reading the paper. He has been interested enough in what interests Steven, engaged enough, to recognise Sirleen Clark – the Mighty Maggot.

That's what makes a good support worker.

The Wasteland

January 2, 2017

My friend was just telling me I missed a treat yesterday because throughout the day Radio Four had Jeremy Irons reading the works of T S Elliott. It reminded me of one of the more surreal moments in the Cowley house last year.

Steven had just put on his Cats DVD. It was the first time the support worker had seen it. After about 10 minutes in, he said to me:

"Ah! Is this the one based on T S Elliott's poems?"

Before I had a chance to reply, Steven chipped in:

"Yes. T S Elliott's Wasteland"

The support worker visibly jumped out of his seat.

Ten minutes later, he followed me into the kitchen and said:

"How on earth does Steven know Elliott wrote The Wasteland?"

"Go and ask him," I replied.

Off he went and I listened but the support worker wasn't quite phrasing the question right, so wasn't getting an answer.

I popped my head round the door and said,

"Steve. Tell Michael. Who was doing T S Elliott, The Wasteland talking?"

Steven replied in a flash:

"Neil Tennant".

After mopping the support worker down with a moist flannel I explained to him that Steven has one of those talking heads videos, The Greatest Number One Singles Of All Time. When they get to number 68, the interviewer asks Neil Tennant how the idea of West End Girls came about, to which Tennant pretentiously replies:

"We were trying to create a collage of voices. We were very much inspired by T S Elliott's The Wasteland. We wanted to create something with that vibe".

Never let it be said we don't do the classics in Cowley.

Arfur Scissorhands

This year's Christmas at Cowley is being sponsored by 1987.

Steven never asks for more than two Christmas presents. Any more than two and they all get lumped together under Steven's special category – "Lovely Surprises". Even though they are "lovely", the additional presents don't command his attention and too many lovely surprises is likely to lead to a sensory overload and potential challenging turkey behaviour.

A few weeks back Steven asked for his first present:

"Dad. Edward Scissorhands video. Present for Christmas day".

And later, to make sure I hadn't missed the salient point:

"Dad. The Edward Scissorhands video. Not the DVD. The video in the white box".

That present wasn't too hard to track down. A bargain £2.85 on Amazon.

The second one was a bit more tricky. With December nearly upon us, Steven watched two Top of The Pops Two Christmas Specials over the weekend. (On VHS). The first one had all the obvious suspects on. The second one drew on more obscure tracks. And it was whilst we were in the middle of the most obscure, that the second present request came in:

"Dad. Dennis Waterman and George Cole. What Are We Going To Get For 'Er Indoors? Christmas present?"

I didn't even know that Minder had spawned a Christmas hit.

Back to Amazon. Only one copy available. Vinyl. £10.75. From Germany. (Apparently in Germany Dennis & George give Boney M a run for their money in the popularity stakes). Fingers crossed. It's due to be delivered between 1st and 20th December.

This morning I popped into Uxbridge on some errands. Dawdling through the market, I spotted a Sony Walkman. Steven used to love wandering from room to room listening to his Walkman. We made him a little handle strap and he used to carry it, elbow bent, rather like Mrs Thatcher used to carry her handbag.

Sod it, I thought. We might as well go the whole hog with our 1980s revival. So I brought it.

It'll be a lovely surprise.

Bristol Fashion

I love Steven's use and understanding of language. Listen to him speak some times and you'd swear he was from the 1950s. Even though, some words throw him, especially if they have two meanings ("Better" for example), once he's grasped a whole phrase, or saying, he just gets it. I don't think I've ever had to explain to him what "Gordon Bennett" means but you often hear the refrain – "Oh! Gordon Bennett" from the kitchen if he's spilled a drink.

One of my favourites he learned courtesy of Mr Crockett, the garage mechanic in Camberwick Green. Mr Crockett had been clearing up the forecourt of the garage and Brian Cant, the narrator, asked him: "Is everything all ship shape and Bristol fashion?" Steven was immediately interested in what this meant and I told him it meant that things were tidy and in order. So now, every evening, as Steven puts his dirty washing in the machine, we ask him "How's things Steve?" To which he replies, "Washing is all ship shape and Bristol fashion". And then we gather around the wireless, with our Double Diamonds and bars of Five Boys chocolate and listen to Round The Horne, before retiring to bed underneath the eiderdown.

I've been trying manfully to get the personal Budget all ship shape and Bristol fashion. I've had a running correspondence with HMRC for the past month about what they saw as a shortfall in the National Insurance I've paid for the support workers' wages. At first, they said the deficit was over £1000. Then they got it down to £532. This morning I got two letters, both dated 2nd February. The first letter states that they have "calibrated" their records and I don't owe them anything. The second letter asks me for £596.28. I immediately panic and start the imagine the bailiffs coming in and removing my collection of Allo Allo DVDs. I then take a closer look at the letter and see that it is stating this figure is their "estimated charges raised for moths 7,8,9 in the absence of you supplying actual figures". This is obviously payment for the third quarter. The third quarter, of which I submitted the tax return three weeks ago. Do I phone them and suggest they have another recalibration of their records?

The same thing happens with the Personal Budget audit that I have to send to the council. Most months, I get a threatening reminder before the forms are due that late return of the audit could result in the personal budget being suspended. You may remember the time that I got a really aggressive phone call from the direct payments manager as there were two cab receipts missing out of a total of 78. Payments of the Personal Budget into the bank account are invariably late. And once I've submitted the returns, I never hear anything for months ("we're working to a backlog"). But for some reason this is okay. I have to be all ship shape and Bristol fashion. But the State can be all haphazard and Newport Pagnellshire fashion.

One expression that Steven can't get his head around is "I'll give them the sharp edge of my tongue" but that's precisely what I'd like to do with these bureaucrats.

P.S.

I've got things all ship shape and Bristol fashion for Steven's birthday next month. Steven has 26 Mr Bean DVDs & 17 Mr Bean videos. There really aren't anymore to buy. It's all the same twelve episodes but in different sleeves. Last week, I was browsing Amazon and noticed there was an American boxed set available. We'll worry about the different region later. Anyway, it arrived today and it's got all the Mr Bean Comic Relief sketches on that don't appear on any of the British versions. What a hero I'll be on the 19th March. Gordon chuffing Bennett.

A Sunday Joke

"Dad – I've got a massive joke"

"That's	right,	that's	right.	that's	right.	that's	right
I	really		love	your		tiger	light
That's	neat,	that's	neat,	that's	neat,	that's	neat

I really love your Richard Madeley"

Fire! F-F-F-Fire!

November 29, 2013

Steven had a great lesson at school when he was about 11 about fire safety. He was really engaged by the messages and would tell anyone keen to listen about how you should manage a fire in your home. And of course, he has also learned a lot about this subject from that other great expert of fire safety – Basil Fawlty.

A good friend of mine brought us a great housewarmming present. It is one of those monster steam irons that looks like it belongs in Aladdin. It pumps out incredible amounts of steam, so much so that my kitchen, on ironing day, resembles a Meat Loaf video.

On Tuesday, Steven's support worker was in the kitchen doing a pile of ironing. Steven was in the living room watching Countdown and I was upstairs writing Christmas cards. All of a sudden I heard a loud but calm voice from downstairs – "EVERYBODY OUT NOW PLEASE". I rushed downstairs to find Steven leading the support worker by the arm into the garden. The kitchen looked like a sauna. Steven saw me and ordered: "Outside please Dad – Fire. F-F-F-Fire".

I explained to him that it was just steam from the iron and that we could go safely back indoors. He wasn't sure, perhaps fearing he'd be sent to his doom like Manuel. The resolution was as follows:

Me: "It's   not   fire   Steve.   It's   only   steam".
Steven: "Steam?   Like   East   17?"
Me: "Yep. Steam like East 17"

And so, in keeping with our life as one long musical, we now have a musical signature tune for any ironing session. Over to you Anthony Mortimer.......

Forever

It was 8 years ago yesterday that Steven was taken from his home. This time of year always triggers the most distressing anxiety. This is how we spent two hours this afternoon. I was expected to repeat back every sentence by way of reassurance. It was accompanied by sobbing, punching his own head and ripping his shirt.

"Watch red Mr Bean video in the Cowley house forever. Watch the blue Mr Bean video in the Cowley house forever. Watch the green Mr Bean video in the Cowley house forever. Watch the purple Mr Bean video in the Cowley house forever. Watch the yellow Mr Bean video in the Cowley house forever. Watch the black Mr Bean video in the Cowley house forever. Watch the pink Mr Bean video in the Cowley house forever. Watch Mr Bean in America video in the Cowley house forever. Watch the Mr Bean's Holiday DVD in the Cowley house forever. Watch the Mr Bean's best bits video in the Cowley house forever. Watch the red Fawlty Towers video in the Cowley house forever. Watch the brown Fawlty Towers video in the Cowley house forever. Watch the green Fawlty Towers video in the Cowley house forever. Watch the blue Fawlty Towers video in the Cowley house forever. Watch Mrs Doubtfire DVD in the Cowley house forever. Watch Grease DVD in the Cowley house forever. Watch Cry Baby DVD in the Cowley house forever. Watch the Full Monty DVD in the Cowley house forever. Watch Muriel's Wedding DVD in the Cowley house forever. Watch Priscilla DVD in the Cowley house forever. Watch Toy Story 1 DVD in the Cowley house forever. Watch Toy Story 2 DVD in the Cowley house forever. Watch Toy Story 3 DVD in the Cowley house forever. Watch The Erasure DVD in the Cowley house forever. Watch The Proclaimers video in the Cowley house forever. Watch The Pet Shop Boys DVD in the Cowley house forever. Watch the Abba Gold DVD in the Cowley house. Watch the Abba DVD with Pete Waterman in the Cowley house forever. Watch the Abba video with Neil Pearson in the Cowley house forever. Watch Mama Mia DVD in the Cowley house forever. Watch the Abba puppets DVD in the Cowley house forever. Watch the blue Beautiful South video in the Cowley house forever. Watch the Beautiful South video with Love Wars in the Cowley house forever. Watch the green Beautiful South DVD in the Cowley house forever. Watch the brown Beautiful South DVD in the Cowley house forever. Watch the Enrique on his motorbike DVD in the Cowley house forever. Watch the Tears For Fears DVD in the Cowley house forever. Watch the Spandau Ballet DVD in the Cowley house forever. Watch the Cher DVD in the Cowley house forever. Watch the Darts DVD in the Cowley house forever. Watch the Mika DVD in the Cowley house forever. Watch the Keane DVD in the Cowley house forever. Watch the Spice Girls DVD in the Cowley house forever. Watch the Shania Twain DVD in the Cowley house forever. Watch the Soft Cell DVD in the Cowley house forever. Watch The Sweet three DVDS in the Cowley house forever. Watch the Elvis Costello DVD in the Cowley house forever. Watch The Jam DVD in the Cowley house forever. Watch The Style Council DVD in the Cowley house forever. Watch The Christians video in the Cowley house forever. Watch the Busted DVD in the Cowley house forever. Watch the Travis DVD in the Cowley house forever. Watch the Anastasia DVD in the Cowley house forever. Watch the Lightning Seeds' video in the Cowley house forever. Watch the Elton John at his show DVD in the Cowley house forever. Watch the Adam Ant DVD in the Cowley house forever. Watch the white Kate Bush video in the Cowley house forever. Watch the Will Young DVD in the Cowley house forever. Watch the Duran Duran DVD in the Cowley house forever. Watch the David Bowie DVD in the Cowley house forever. Watch the Kirsty McColl DVD in the Cowley house forever. Watch the white Live Aid DVD in the Cowley house forever. Watch the blue Live Aid DVD in the Cowley house forever. Watch the Boney M DVD in the Cowley house forever. Watch the Bryan Adams show DVD in the Cowley house forever. Watch the Fatboy Slim DVD in the Cowley house forever. Watch the little Housemartins DVD in the Cowley house forever. Watch the little Pet Shop Boys DVD in the Cowley house forever. Watch the little Right Said Fred DVD in the Cowley house forever. Watch all the Men Behaving Badly videos in the Cowley house forever. Watch all The Gladiators videos in the Cowley house forever. Watch all the Good Life DVDS in the Cowley house forever. Watch the all the people singing Abba songs video in the Cowley house forever. Watch the Grangewood Christmas Show video with Steven Neary in Bananas in pyjamas in the Cowley house forever. Watch the Grangewood Christmas Show video with Steven Neary in Walking through the jungle in the Cowley house forever. Watch the Grangewood Christmas Show video with Steven Neary in Walking on the Moon in the Cowley house forever. Watch the Grangewood Christmas Show video with Steven Neary in Cats in the Cowley house forever. Watch the red Coronation Street video with Rita and Mavis and Alec on the boat in the Cowley house forever. Watch the blue EastEnders video with Phil and Grant taking their clothes off in the Cowley house forever. Do massive music tapes with Dad on Saturday in the Cowley house forever. Do massive music tapes with Dad on Sunday in the Cowley house forever. Talk to Dad in the living room in the Cowley house forever. Talk to Dad in the kitchen in the Cowley house forever. Alan will cook your chicken pie on Thursday night in the

Cowley house forever. Go to Jay's sweet shop on Friday and Saturday and Sunday in the Cowley house forever. Go to bed in the Cowley house forever. Do a poo in the Cowley house forever. Have my lovely surprise in the Cowley house forever. Not going to a house with stairs. Staying in the Cowley house with no stairs forever".

Happy New Year.

The Kiki Dee Conundrum

It's going to be a long day. Steven has discovered a new life conundrum.

He's always been fascinated by actors playing different roles. The prime example of this for him is Rowan Atkinson. Steven loves and is fascinated by the fact that Mr Atkinson has been Mr Bean, Black Adder, Johnny English, The Rude Vicar. Steven likes to sort of the chronology of roles so we often have conversations that go:

"Rowan Atkinson was Mr Bean first. Then Rowan Atkinson went to play Johnny English".

He likes to keep the support workers on their toes by deliberately getting it wrong and waiting for them to correct him —

"Chris — Rowan Atkinson was Johnny English first. Then he went to Mr Bean?" He finds this hysterical and waits in anticipation whilst the support worker consults his internal Wikipedia.

Steven does the same thing with John Cleese ("John Cleese went to Basil Fawlty first. Then he went to Donald Sinclair") and Martin Clunes ("Martin Clunes went to Gary Strang first. Then he went to Churchill").

Another variation on this theme is cover versions, which hold an endless curiosity. As I type, Steven is doing a music session and has included lots of covers. He's listening to Kim Wilde's version of "If I Can't Have You" and teasing the support worker with — "Chris — Yvonne Elleman sings a Kim Wilde song". Thankfully, Chris is on the ball and knows that it is the other way round. This kind of conundrum can provide Steven with endless hours of amusement. And the more cover versions the better. He can really go to town on the number of versions we've got of Unchained Melody.

But today has thrown up a new dilemma. Steven has known the soundtrack to Blood Brothers for years. I had the 1995 cast recording and he's known that the woman who sings Tell Me It's Not True is called Mrs Johnstone. With all the characters, he's accepted them by their character name. In 2002 we went on holiday to Bournemouth and whilst there we went to see the touring version of Blood Brothers. During Act 1 we had the potentially meltdown inducing conversation:

"Dad – Mrs Johnstone looks a bit like Linda Nolan".

"It is Linda Nolan Steve. Linda Nolan is playing Mrs Johnstone".

Thankfully Steven accepted that and since whenever he listens to the CD, he talks about Linda Nolan playing the mother.

At the weekend I found my copy of the 1989 cast recording. This is when Kiki Dee was playing Mrs Johnstone. Cue confusion:

"Dad. Linda Nolan's not singing this song."

"No Steve. It's Kiki Dee playing Mrs Johnstone".

"Dad's doing silly talking. Two ladies playing Mrs Johnstone. That's too greedy".

"Not greedy Steve. Kiki Dee went to Blood Brothers. Then Kiki Dee left and Linda Nolan came".

I think I got away with it. I've just heard him say to Chris – "Chris – Kiki Dee went to Blood Brothers first. Then Kiki Dee went to Elton John?"

I might have got away with it for the time being but I'm going to keep to myself the fact that Mel C also played Mrs Johnstone. In fact, to quote another Blood Brother's song, I'm Not Saying A Word.

A Cowley Man

This is just going to be a factual narrative of the last two days – I'm too exhausted to write any other way (I'm slightly worried that I'm knackered and we haven't even started yet.

Yesterday afternoon, I spent the best part of two hours in the Civic Centre signing a mountain of forms and contracts. I was given the keys, parted with the first month's rent and wished all the best for Steven's new home.

So, on arriving home, for the first time since this all blew up last September, I was able to give Steven some concrete information. He was over the moon and danced around the room for about 10 minutes. I was cooking tea when his support worker returned for the evening shift and I heard Steven tell him:

"Uncle Wayne's a Cowley man.
David is a Cowley man
Lee is a Cowley man
Dave is a Cowley man
Patrick is a Cowley man
STEVEN NEARY IS A COWLEY MAN NOW"

This morning I arrived at the house early with my sister to open up for Steven's first viewing. They only gave me one key yesterday which turned out to be the back door key. I must have tried the front lock over a dozen times and for a split second, entertained the thought that perhaps squatters had moved in. My sister phoned David, her son and announced "me and Uncle Mark are too old to climb over the wall" and David arrived to save the day ten minutes later.

It was good to look round the house without all the housing people present and I started to visualise where everything would go. The state of the living room carpet became all too apparent – our feet kept sticking to it! The whole house needs decorating quite frankly but there is time to do that before we have to vacate the flat. The first week in November started to show up in my head for the actual move. My sister has assembled a decorating team and it should look beautiful in two weeks time.

Steven and the support workers turned up and he was really engaged and jolly as we went from room to room. Steven is a lazy buggar and I think he'd been pinning his hopes that he'd have a maisonette like Uncle Wayne – the stairs were the only things that didn't impress him.

After they left, we went off to buy the cooker, fridge and washing machine and all the paint (another £900 of the damages bites the dust).

Home an hour later than I would normally on a Tuesday, Steven was on edge and that has continued since. Lots of changes. Routines broken. Uncertainty now for the next two and a half weeks. It's going to be a very hairy fortnight. I tried to go upstairs to phone the electricity people (there is no gas or electric at the moment) but couldn't get anywhere for the meltdown taking place downstairs. I think this is why I already feel worn out – there is so much to do but I get so little time (about 6 hours per week) when I'm either not working or caring for Steven. I've tried to do a list of priorities but even that looks too much to do in the short space of time I get free.

In amongst all this, I've been trying to deal with several phone calls and emails. Victoria Derbyshire wants to interview me about the move on Radio 5 Live tomorrow, so as well as the pre interview questions, they were having to arrange a radio car to come to the flat (there is no way I could travel up to Oxford Circus with so much going on). It's odd because it will be nearly three years to the day since Victoria interviewed me the day after Steven made his escape from the positive behaviour unit. And it's almost a year to the day since she interviewed me as I sat in my pants in a Leeds' hotel room after we received the news of my housing benefit stopping. I've been invited to speak at the House of Lords Committee looking into the Mental Capacity Act, so tried to arrange the dates for that. Plus, I've had two speaking engagement offers and need to book hotel and travel for those.

The support worker clocked off at 6pm and Steven has settled into his regular 2 hour Tuesday night music DVD session. Except he keeps calling me downstairs every five minutes to check out the latest anxious thought that pops into his head:

"Dad – put The Beautiful South CDs in a box?"
"Dad – put trunks in the holiday suitcase?"
"Dad – still have steak in the Cowley house?"
"Dad – not going back to M house (the unit) – Cowley house is forever and ever?"

Thankfully, I can answer "yes" to all those questions. And between now and the first week in November, I expect to have to answer the same questions and a thousand like it many times.

I had a big thought yesterday. Three years ago Hillingdon were planning on moving Steven to a hospital in Wales for "further assessment" as to why his behaviour was so challenging at the unit. Three years on, after three court hearings, many more battles, Steven has got a home of his home. It's chilling to know that Steven came within a breath of, as Justice Peter Jackson put it, "facing a life in care that he does not want or does not need".

Steven Neary & The Great Works of Art
September 16, 2013

Since the beginning of the summer, Steven has been coming to my workplace every Monday. I work in a beautiful 18th century building. It was originally a farm house, then a family home and is now home to the local Arts Centre. I rent the library 4 days a week for my counselling practice. Steven uses the music room. He very quickly established a routine – he takes a C90 tape that we prepared the day before. At the halfway point of the tape, he stops for a cherry bakewell and an orange juice. After the tape, Steven and one of his support workers have a sing song around the piano. The I pop to the local cafe and get bacon sandwiches for all for lunch. We then sit in the beautiful maze garden and wait for the cab to take us home.

Steven loves it.

He also quickly made a friend as well. Every other Monday, an art group use the room next to the music room and Steven likes an elderly chap who teaches the group. Today, we were sitting in the garden, waiting for the car, when Steven spotted hs friend leaving.

"Bye Raj"

Raj came over and they shook hands. Steven showed Raj the spot on his hand and got very excited when Raj told him not to pick it in case he got blood all over the bench.

The following conversation took place:

Raj: "Do you know Steven that I'm a painting teacher"

Steven: "A painting teacher".

Raj: "And because you're such a good man, I'm going to do you a painting. What would you like me to do you a painting of?"

Steven: "Whistler's Mother"

Raj looked at me:

Raj: "Sorry, what did he say?"

Me: "He said he would like you to paint him Whistler's Mother"

Raj: "That's what I thought he said. Do you know Whistler's Mother Steven?"

Steven: "She's a hideous old bat who looks like she's had a cactus stuffed up her backside".

At this point, we had to stop Raj falling backwards into the rose bush. We explained the plot of Mr Bean in America and Raj left like a man with a mission.

I do believe that we're going to get a copy of Whistler's Mother to hang in our new home.

None of that would have happened if Steven had been taken to a hospital in Wales.

How To Make A Life

April 16, 2018

I often feel a bit teary when I get back to my flat on a Sunday evening after spending the weekend with Steven. If the weekend had been problematic, I feel sad that the precious time had been spoiled. Or, if the weekend has been pretty damn perfect I get a bit emotional because … we'll, because the weekend had been pretty damn perfect.

This weekend has been pretty damn perfect and I've been trying to understand why. The other day, one of my clients threw into the session, "I don't think I was ever taught how to make a life". What ensued was an existential discussion on what "making" a life actually means and can you be taught how to do it.

I marvel at how Steven makes his life. To an outside commentator it may look a pretty small life. But to someone who loves him, I hear a noise he makes. It's hard to describe in words. The best I can come up with is it's like a purr. A purr of total contentment. We spent quite a bit of time doing what Steven calls a "two songs" compilation tape. It's cover versions basically. I brought him some cover versions CDs for his birthday. Some absolute corkers – James Blunt doing I Guess That's Why They Call It The Blues and Kylie Minogue doing Bette Davis Eyes. On the tape yesterday I put on two versions of Just The Way You Are. First Billy Joel, then Barry White. Steven loves the Barry version. "Dad – do Barry White" he asked. This involves a vocal and physical impersonation. So I affect my most gravely voice and mop my sweaty face with a hanky. This brings about " the purr". And Steven skips off into the hall, announcing "Don't you just love Barry White".

Music does make Steven's life. I always announce I'm going off to bed about 10pm because if I didn't, Steven would have me up all night chatting about this, that and the other. He goes about his business for another hour and then announces to the support worker that he is off to bed too. On Saturday night, I heard him say, "Michael. I'm off to bed now. And I'm going to be singing some Liam Gallagher". And for the next hour or so, you can hear from his bedroom – "Maybe, I don't really want to know…" That makes me and Michael purr.

Is this making a life? I guess so. It definitely feels like living a life. It requires some outside input (i.e. me buying the James Blunt and Kylie CD) but I don't think it can be taught. It's too spontaneous for that.

Anyway, enough of the philosophy. Get those hankies out and swallow some gravel:

"Tonight Matthew. I'm going to be…."

A Human Uncle

Have a look at this photo. Tell me what you see. It was taken on Thursday when Uncle Wayne came to do some jobs around Steven's new house. The young chap in the photo is Henry, Wayne's grandson. When Henry was born, Steven was over the moon that he had now become an "uncle". Technically, Steven and Henry are second cousins but Steven sees being an uncle as very much part of being a man, so he's become an honorary uncle:

After the guests went home, me and one of the support workers popped out to get fish and chips and the worker suddenly said, "This is one of the happiest days of my working life". He explained that he was moved by Steven being such an adult and being gentle and interested in Henry. Later, after posting the photo on Facebook, someone commented, "You should send this photo to Justice Peter Jackson. Let him know he made the right decision all those years ago". Both comments had me welling up. The photo captures a tiny moment in time. A short period where Steven will be the "adult" in a relationship. In a couple of years time, Henry will sail straight past Steven and that will be that. Normal positions resumed. Henry cried when it came to time to go home because he didn't want to leave. Steven had a meltdown later in the evening because he wanted Uncle Wayne and Henry to come back. What could be more human than that?

Will Young & Nappies

October 20, 2013

Every Saturday afternoon since Steven was 11, we've done a C90 compilation tape. Back in the day, it was preparation for his walkman that he used to listen to at playtime at school. These days, he listens to the tape back on Sunday mornings with his support workers, giving me a chance for a lay in.

This is how the conversation went with his support worker earlier:

"What's this song Steve?"

"Poetry in Motion by Johnny Tillotson"

"It sounds like a very old song".

"Very old song. Mark Neary was sitting on Nanny Beryl's lap with his nappy on".

"And where was Steven Neary?"

"Steven Neary was not here yet".

The following track was "Leave Right Now" by Will Young.

"Did Mark Neary still have his nappy on for Will Young?"

Cue hysterical laughter from Steven......

"Nick's doing silly talking. Mark Neary is a man for Will Young"

"And where was Steven Neary?"

"In David Watson's class. Doing modern foreign languages"

A Single Munchie

February 14, 2014

This works for me on many levels.

Steven was sitting on the sofa, watching Deal or No Deal and eating a packet of Munchies. His support worker, who he has a great laugh with was darning one of his socks.

M: Go on Steve – let me have one of your Munchies.

Steve: No thank you.

M: Ah – it could be my special prize for a good swim today.

Steve: A special prize?

Long pause for thought. Steven puts a single Munchie on the arm of the sofa.

Steve: Michael wants a special prize. No Munchie yet.

Another long pause whilst Steven works out his question.......

Steve: Michael – Simply Red sang a Harold Melvin & The Bluenotes song. It was a song called?...........

Sadly, Michael didn't know the answer, so Steven ate the last Munchie himself.

To get a prize in the Cowley house, you need a thorough knowledge of pop music.

Dad's Doing Silly Talking

September 11, 2016

Last night, Steven told me off. It was brilliant. It was humbling. I don't think it's ever happened before. I felt one inch tall. I went back in time 46 years to that day at summer camp where I boasted to my friends that I could do "really cool reggae dancing" to Double Barrel by Dave & Ansil Collins. And my world came tumbling down as I did my cool reggae dancing and Sharon Martyn laughed.

Steven and I were doing a music dvd session and watching The Pet Shop Boys & Dusty Springfield. Steven has always seem to have had a very straight forward understanding of death. The deceased has a "bad" something or other. And when we've agreed which part of their body has gone "bad", he follows it up with his certainty that it's gone bad because they "bashed it" on something. I don't think he understands how things can go wrong internally without being bashed. We bash things and if we're unlucky, that leads to death.

He's had a black toenail for a couple of days after catching his foot on the edge of the fridge. I don't think he's thought that he's going to die. But the sequence of events work for Steven. Bashed his toe on the fridge – pain – bruised foot.

Yes. Dusty Springfield. Steven has known for ages that she died. This is how the conversation went:

Steven: Dad – Dusty Springfield's died.

Me: Yes mate. Dusty Springfield has died.

Steven: Dusty Springfield had a bad chest.

Me: Yes mate. Dusty Springfield had a bad chest.

Steven: Bashed her chest on the ......?

Me: Bashed her chest on the garden gate mate.

Steven: That's silly talking Dad. Talk sensible.

I was stopped in my tracks. Have we entered a new phase in our relationship? Have my autopsy reports been spotted for the fraud they are? Is it time to go

in for proper medical reasons?

Steven: Can't bash her chest on the garden gate. Garden gate is too small. Dusty Springfield bashed her chest on the floor when she fell off the comfy chair.

I didn't want to argue that the living room floor is even lower than the garden gate. Dr Neary was satisfied with his diagnosis.

All this talk of silly talking took me back to 2010 and the visit from the Speech Therapist to teach me and two support workers how to talk to Steven. She had decided that Steven didn't understand sentences with more than four words in. And when it came to instructions, every vowel had to be "stretched out like a piece of plasticine". She wanted to observe us supporting Steven whilst he made some cheese on toast. When it got to the part of me saying, "Put cheeeese on bread", Steven looked at me quizzically and said, "Dad's doing silly talking". The therapist chuckled and said, "Oh bless him. It might take a while for Steven to get used to this new communication". I chuckled back in an embarrassed fashion whereas what I really should have said was, "No. Steven is spot on. This is silly talking. Excuse me a minute. Steve – you know how to make cheese on toast don't you? You get on and do it and I'll go and watch Loose Women".

I wish I could talk like Steven. I wish I could cut straight through the nonsense. Instead of saying how it really is, I bumble and stutter and try to be tactful. It never works. And I end up furious with myself for being so incongruent.

New home. No more plasticine.

The Hard Drive
July 11, 2017

The only downside of Steven coming off the medication has been that it takes him so much longer to find the words he wants to say. I understand the mechanics. The anti psychotics slowed everything down, making retrieval from his mental hard drive relatively straight forward. Now that he is no longer chemically coshed, everything has sped up and moving at a speed that Steven is unused to.

This morning he called me into the kitchen to have a chat. It took fifteen minutes of thumbing through the files on his hard drive to locate what he wanted to talk about. In that fifteen minutes, he was muttering as he browsed his "language files" and I was fascinated in how things were ordered.

This is how it went:

"Mr Rumpling on his boat in Chigley.

Anastasia with her glasses on.

No, you can't speak to Uncle Wayne on the phone. Uncle Wayne's gone fishing.

Anthony Mortimer kicked the candle in the church in Gold.

Ken Barlow's dog called Eccles.

Jet doesn't go to Gladiators anymore. Jet's got a bad neck.

Can't eat 10 chocolate biscuits. That's too greedy.

Dr Mo has got bleed on her hands in Holby City.

Alvin Stardust.

Martin Clunes on his motorbike with Churchill.

Gareth Gates looks like Logan in the gym.

Get some Fruit Pastilles in Jay's shop on Friday.

Harold Melvin's got very big hair.

DAD! SYBIL FAWLTY IS DRIVING OVER TO BABBACOMBE. LIKE CHRIS".

That was it. One of the support workers is on holiday this week in Babbacombe. Steven was excited about this and wanted to share the connection he'd made.

But what a journey through the hard drive to reach that point.

Dreams of Gabrielle

April 18, 2015

With the toothache not totally cured and the DVD player of the new TV playing up, there is a slightly tense atmosphere in the Cowley house.

Thank goodness for Steven's grand flights of fantasy to relieve the tension.

This afternoon, we were watching a Top of the Pops celebration of the nineties. Up pops Gabrielle, singing Dreams. As ever, Steven is keen to develop a back story……

"Gabrielle's got a patch on her eye.

Gabrielle bashed her eye on a twig.

Gabrielle was in the woods at night-time.

Gabrielle had left her torch in the kitchen.

Gabrielle's husband said Gabrielle can't go indoors because Gabrielle said a rude word.

Gabrielle – you don't want to be blind like Andrea Bocelli.

Twigs are massive sharp and dangerous.

Gabrielle – go to Holby City & let Dr Elliott get the jip out of your eye.

Steven Neary's not going in the woods at night-time. Steven Neary is staying indoors to watch Mr Robbie Lewis and Mr James Hathaway."

He was still telling the story of Gabrielle's accident when the programme had moved on to The Manic Street Preachers.

Trevor

Forgive me. I'm feeling a bit of an emotional old Hector this evening.

Steven went to Virgin Active for about four years. He used to love standing on the periphery of the water aerobics group and singing along to In The Navy. He made lots of friends there. People like John, and Tony and Malcolm, that he still talks about. The person who made the biggest impact on him was Trevor. Trevor was in his early eighties at the time. They used to meet in the changing rooms. Steven would arrive as Trevor was leaving. Steven used to show Trevor his latest spot, or scratch and Trevor's response always made Steven laugh – "Take care of that spot young Steven".

Then one day, Steven had a meltdown in reception and lashed out at Trevor. Thankfully he didn't make contact but it led to Steven receiving a lifetime ban from the club. Trevor was mortified and tried to speak up on Steven's behalf but the manager refused to back down.

At the time it felt like their relationship was going the same way as most of Steven's relationships – nice whilst they last but they never last for long.

That was in the spring of 2012. That Christmas Trevor phoned me. He'd tracked down our number and asked if he could come and see Steven at Christmas. He arrived with a box of biscuits and Steven was over the moon. About the biscuits. And about seeing his old friend. The first thing Steven did was to show Trevor a newly picked scab on his leg.

Every Christmas since, Trevor has turned up the week before Christmas with the biscuits. Even last year. We moved in October but Trevor phoned social services to find out where Steven had gone.

He phoned an hour ago to arrange this year's visit. We chatted and he told me his wife had been in hospital four times this year, including two strokes. She was admitted for the fourth time last weekend. I told him he had enough on his plate and not to worry this year. Trevor wouldn't hear of it. He's too fond of Steven and doesn't want to disappoint him.

I could never tell this story to the professionals. They'd side with the manager of Virgin Active and be consumed by risk assessing. They would reduce Steven and Trevor's relationship to a circle of support.

I guess there's a 60 year age difference between Steven and Trevor.

Their relationship is quietly beautiful. I wouldn't want that contaminated.

Friends With Briefcases.

May 24, 2015

I've got a bit of a lump in my throat this morning.

One of the support workers told me a story about a mate of his who is employed by a care agency. One of the mate's jobs is to go into a residential unit and take a young guy to the gym. Last week the manager of the unit contacted the manager of the agency expressing concern about the mate breaking professional boundaries. He was suspended pending an LA investigation. What did he do? It was the client's 30th birthday. His only family, his brother, was out of the country. Knowing that nobody at the unit would acknowledge the birthday, the mate went to visit his client with a card and present. It was his day off. He was called into the manager's office, and this is the bit that chokes me up, was reminded that he is not a friend and had crossed a professional boundary. Had he?

Steven's thoughts are very much on his holiday at the moment. This morning he was running through the plans for the day we arrive. I'd already told him that I would have to go out for the shopping, so he said, "Steven Neary will do some swimming with his friends". Am I meant to correct him on this? " No Steven. Alan and Das are not your friends. They are your employees".

I'll always remember how the social worker, in her statement for court, put the words Steven's friends in inverted commas. It expressed incredulity that he might have friends. It also felt slightly mocking. This othering of a learning disabled person's experience is why I shudder at terms like Circles of Support. It distances. My friends don't need a one page profile of me to reacquaint themselves with before we meet up.

Later Steven will go off to the Mencap Pool. When he gets back and I ask him who he saw there, he'll say "Steven Neary's friends" and will reel off a list of names of people he saw there. Should I tell him that Richard and Jean are not friends – they run the pool. What about Tyler, his personal trainer at the gym? Steven sees him as a friend because Tyler will sing Proclaimers songs whilst they are doing a chest press.

My friends are my friends for some simple reasons. I like them and they like me. I care about them and they care about me. I'm interested in them and they're interested in me. We make each other laugh. That's it. Odd though it may seem on Planet Social Care, Steven's relationships are built on pretty much the same foundations.

Steven is sharp. He relates very differently to someone who turns up with a briefcase or a file. He senses the interaction is different. He doesn't include the briefcases in his collection of friends. I'm not sure how he categorizes them but they're not on his friends radar. They occupy a different space in his taxonomy.

As I write, Steven is listening to his Sunday tape with his support worker. They've just had a song from Blood Brothers that Mickey and Eddie sing. The first line is "My best friend always has sweets to share". In a minute, they'll go off together to the shop to get some milk, the papers, a bag of Frazzles for Steven and a caramac for the support worker. Same routine every Sunday. When they get back, the support worker will break his caramac in two and share it with Steven. They'll eat it together whilst discussing dead pop stars.

Perhaps I should buy the support worker a briefcase for his caramac.

Compare & Contrast

June 7, 2014

On Wednesday, I wrote a post for the #107days blog called "The Cast". I've no idea why but for some reason, it has attracted four times the views of any other of 81 posts I've written as part of the campaign. It was quite a simple post, where I listed all the people appointed by Hillingdon during 2010 to work on Steven's case. The list was as follows:

1 social worker
1 social work manager
1 support planner
1 transition manager
1 Head of Services
1 Head of Residential services
1 Positive behaviour support manager
1 Deputy positive behaviour support manager
4 psychiatrists
1 keyworker
1 linkworker
2 psychologists
4 best interests assessors
1 Safeguarding lead for DoLs
6 Locum borough solicitors
3 speech and language therapists
1 Learning Disability Community nurse
2 Occupational therapists
approx 20 Unit support workers
1 Dietitian
And the commissioned agency on a 100% mark up for every hour they provided a support worker to work with Steven.

Since Wednesday, I've been observing Steven going about his business and been struck between the contrast of all those professionals who think they have something valuable to add, and how Steven is capable of managing his time and doing what interests him. The last week has been potentially tough because several of the normal, reliable routines have gone out of the window. I've taken the week off work to get on with sorting out the funeral, all the paperwork and the old marital home. So, I've been around at home more than

I would be, especially on Thursday and Friday. Also, the health club where Steven goes for his Tuesday and Thursday spa is closed for refurbishments, so he's had to do alternative activities.

I do find it entertaining, watching Steven entertain himself. He usually doesn't like other people involved when he's doing something unplanned. On Thursday afternoon, I got back from the funeral directors and Steven was perched on a chair in front of the CD player, working his way through his four disc Abba CD set. The support worker told me that he'd been at it for over an hour. All in all, he sat there for three hours, giving a running commentary to himself of each song. Yesterday, I had the horrific task of going back to start sorting out the house. I arrived back home about ten minutes before Steven got back from the day centre. I brought home 14 photo albums, so when Steven got home, he spent the next three hours before swimming, reading through each album. He only called for me when he needed my input for times, like the snap at Weymouth. He pointed to a pinsize man in the distance of the picture and wanted to know what his name was and the colours of his trousers and whether he's been stung on the knee by a jellyfish. There were several of those back stories created during the session. It was the same this morning. I went into Uxbridge to meet my friend Mary and got a phone call from home. Steven had sorted out his Smash Hits 1999 Party video (hosted by Steps) and he wanted to tell me a good H from Steps joke. When I got home at midday, the support worker told me that Steven had been busy all morning – after the video he went off to the computer and spent an hour searching Youtube for clips of Carry On films. The worker told me that he tried to be involved but Steven sent him away with: "Steven Neary wants to do Charlie Hawtrey talking on his own".

I'm really proud he can do all that. When he was in the Unit, they correctly identified that unfilled time and space is problematic for Steven. An autism expert had sent me some stuff about sensory underload, which fitted very much my experience of Steven when he has nothing to do. I found it interesting that an overload or an underlaod, can both easily lead to the same outcome – a meltdown. But what the Unit got terribly wrong was that they couldn't acknowledge that they were creating the unfilled space. All the things I've mentioned above weren't available to Steven – no computer, no DVD player. And the things that were available (a video player), he couldn't use when he wanted to – he had to negotiate the use with staff and other residents. And worse than that, the Unit, and in particular, the social worker, put value judgements on anything Steven did. Creating a story around a photo was seen as valueless, whilst learning to load the washing machine was seen as tremendously valuable.

So, in not providing the opportunities for Steven to get on living his life, or by placing judgements on the things he wanted to do, they then created, what they saw as a need for all that external input. Utterly self serving. They couldn't see that lying on the sofa with nothing to do or nobody to talk to about the things he wanted to talk about set off a meltdown but they employed all those people in trying to find a solution. I have to admit, I still get angry when I think about how, not only was that such an abuse of Steven, but also, what a colossal waste of money and resources.

If any of those people in that list above were to become a fly on our wall, they wouldn't recognise Steven. But then neither, would they see the part they played in that.

Mr Soppy

Steven has a new "feelings" word. Soppy.

For quite a while now, he has been able to identify and name the following feelings: happy, sad, cross and anxious. Now he has added "soppy" to his list.

"Steven Neary's gone a bit soppy" has now become a familiar phrase in his vocabulary. To accompany the statement, he goes red and looks a little sheepish but with a huge grin on his face.

And what makes Steven Neary go a bit soppy?

Jet from Gladiators
Mel B
Suzie Dent
Mary from Coronation Street!!!!
Jay from Bucks Fizz
Sonique
Jo Wiley

It's nice to feel a soppy man

Different Words

"Dad"

"Yes Steve"

"It's Enrique Dad"

"Enrique mate?"

"Steven Neary's got an Enrique song with different words".

"Let's hear it then Steve"

"I will be your hero baby

I will kiss away the pain

I will stand by you forever

You can take my Bernard Cribbens away"

Muriel On The Move

October 1, 2016

As we start our last weekend in the Cowley house (now known as the old Cowley house), here's a few random recollections of the last three weeks.

"Dad – don't forget to put Muriel's Wedding in the box. Going to watch Bill Hislop shouting on Monday night in the new Cowley house".

Life is so much easier when you can deal with someone directly. The minute you add outsourcing into the equation, you disappear into the void. The decorator, the gardener's, the removal company, the TV aerial installation man are all one person businesses and dealing with them has been straightforward and human. On the other hand, take Argos (please take Argos). As is their style, they split my order into two deliveries. One delivery came on time to the right address. The other half was delivered to my flat. I wasn't at my flat – I was waiting for it at the new house, so they left it with my neighbour. Except for one item, the microwave, which they decided my neighbour couldn't be trusted with, so they took it back to the outsourced delivery firm's depot. It took eight days, six phone calls taking 4 1/2 hours to track it down. Hopefully the microwave will now arrive on Monday morning.

" Dad – taking Mr Bean (the life sized cardboard cutout) to the new Cowley house on Sunday morning. Don't want Mr Bean be squashed to death in Luke's moving lorry".

At 57, the time has come to accept that I'm crap at DIY. It's not my forte. I freeze and imagine a Greek chorus laughing at me. I managed to assemble the new armchair (3 parts) and I could screw four legs onto Steven's new sofa. But faced with a new wardrobe, it just seemed less fraught and less likely to be a Frank Spencer moment to leave Wayne and my sister to get on with it whilst I played Thomas the Tank Engine with my great nephew on the newly laid living room carpet.

"Dad – Chris and Alan will be Steven Neary's moving buddies. Like Mr Potato Head".

Roy the decorator worked bloody hard. The living room and my bedroom were in such a state, it took him six coats of paint before the walls and ceilings started to look reasonable. Even now, the temptation to add one more coat is very strong. Trouble is, with so many coats, two of the doors no longer shut. Cue one of the support team, who turned up yesterday morning with his sander and sorted them out. The support workers have been brilliant. I've hardly seen Steven over the past three weeks. But the guys have stepped up and taken so much of the pressure off. And they're all coming in at 8 o'clock on Monday morning to do their bit for the move.

" Dad – they're knocking the walls down in the old Cowley house on Monday. Don't want the bricks to crush Steven Neary's Proclaimers CDs".

Some days the relentless bureaucracy of the world beat me. It seems like the OT has agreed to having a bath installed but wanted a "professional" letter to support my claim. Late last Friday afternoon, I got a call from the GP's surgery to say the letter was ready for collection. I picked it up and was charged £30 for the privilege of the two paragraph letter. When I read it, it was all my own words. It was exactly the same words that I'd said to the GP when requesting it. I took it to the Civic Centre, only to be told they don't do photocopying anymore. I'd have to go the library and queue up again upon my return. Even though the library is only about 600 yards away, I couldn't do it. I gave up and went to the Slug & Lettuce and had a pint and steak & chips instead.

"Dad – say goodbye to Ranjt at the sweet shop on Sunday morning. Got a new sweet shop on Monday morning. With Frazzles. And a Milky Bar".

I'm lucky to have my sister and Wayne. They just get on with things. They don't laugh at me (well, not much). They don't shout at me when I pull the blinds they've spent hours putting up, crashing down. They dealt with the stroppy neighbour who thought 7pm was too late to be drilling six holes for the TV bracket. They just love Steven and are determined to get his home right for him.

" Dad – The Christmas tree. Dad – the Christmas tree. Dad – the Christmas tree. Put the Christmas tree box in a moving box".

A few unanswered questions: Did I crack the TV screen when moving it from my neighbours (Thank you Argos) to the new house or was it already broken? What was that brown sticky stuff caked into several of the kitchen drawers? Will we get a TV signal eventually? Will my bad back survive packing and unpacking? Where will the Mr Bean cardboard cutout go?

"Dad – on Monday morning, Steven Neary & Mark Neary & Alan & Michael & Francis & Des & Chris will sing, 'Oh bright new day, were moving away. We're starting all over again' ".

The Boys Are Back In Town

October 16, 2018

I spent the morning with Steven. It was a fortnight ago today we last hung out together. The plan, pre heart attack, was to meet up last Saturday but everyone felt, post heart attack, that I needed a bit more time.

I arrived just as Steven was getting out of the bath. I think he broke his allcomers record for getting dressed and having breakfast. He had two week's worth of conversations to catch up on.

First up, and in preparation for his DVD viewing this afternoon, he wanted to talk about every track on his Culture Club Greatest Hits collection. Not only does this entail naming every song but describing what Boy George and Jon were wearing in each video.

Then we moved on to the "daily photo" which is where Steven takes one snap out of an album and provides a running commentary of every detail in the photo. Today's choice at face value was a picture of me and Steven sitting on the floor of the living room watching the Exciting Escapades of Mr Bean. Once we've gone through what we're all wearing his attention turns to the videos and books on the bookshelf and we have to name every one. I can sometimes push my luck and when we get to about the 30th video, I say "Oh, I don't know that one" and we move on to what items of food are sitting on the dining room table.

After a break for a drink, I'm summoned into the kitchen as Steven has moved on to his lookalikes game and wants my opinion on who each member of Boyzone resemble amongst the staff at Moorcroft school. (In case you're interested, Keith Duffy looks like Steven's classroom assistant from Class 2, Phil Green, purely on account of him having a pony tail).

Another break for a pee and Steven tells me his joke of the day: "Dad. Morning is broken. That's a silly song Dad. You can break a plate but you can't break a morning".

I pottered back home and haven't moved off the sofa since. All of those conversations took place standing up. I haven't done much conversing or standing up for the past 12 days. I put the TV on but even Escape To The

Country was over stimulating so I laid flat out and watched a bargee attend to his parbuckles. I couldn't summon up the energy to do anything more.

It was nice to be back. And we haven't got on to discussing Christmas yet.

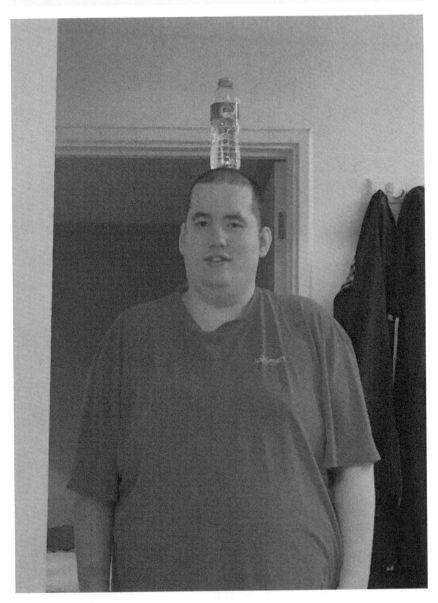

So Many People

I wrote a few weeks back that Steven made a great connection between his meltdown and the trigger for it. It was the day before we were due to go on holiday and he was agitated for nearly six hours and saying that he didn't want to go. Eventually, he was able to say that he didn't want to go on holiday because "holidays get a bit busy".

It was the first time I've ever heard him make a link like that. I was almost tempted to phone the Positive Behaviour Support team! He had sussed why he experiences sensory overload in an amusement arcade, or at the fair, or on a busy beach. And from that point, he was able to structure his holiday precisely to his requirements.

Today he did something similar. The calendar has turned over to July and Steven knows that this is the time quite a few things change. School goes on holiday and the Mencap Pool closes for the duration of the school break. Each year, we have to find an alternative for his Friday night and Sunday morning swims. So, earlier, he was asking about where we will be going instead. I suggested three different places but each suggestion produced a scream and he started to work himself up. I went into the kitchen to leave him to it. About ten minutes later, he came out, having calmed down:

"Dad – don't want to go to Hayes pool 'cos?"

"I dunno mate. Steven Neary doesn't want to go to Hayes pool cos?....."

"Dad – don't want to go to Hayes pool cos song in Peter and Linda film".

"What's the song in the Peter and Linda film mate?" For a few minutes, I wasn't even sure what film he meant, let alone the song.

He went back into the living room and I could hear him talking to himself, trying to remember the words of a song.

Ten minutes later, Tigger bounded into the kitchen:

" Dad – so many people. Peter and Linda song".

Bloody hell. How did he remember that? We used to have a VHS tape of Willie Russell's Dancing Through The Dark. It must have been sixteen years since he's watched it. It was finally released on DVD about a year ago and I got it but Steven has never watched it.

But it was the same as the holiday. Only this time he needed a musical clue to express his feelings. He doesn't want to go to Hayes pool as there are So Many People.

I wish we were all so musical in expressing our unconscious. This week at work, I've had so many people talking about major fall outs with family or friends since the referendum vote. It's like some deep rooted unconscious fear has burst out but expressed in frightened anger. Whatever it is about, it's not the thing that people are arguing about – the impact is too disproportionate to the subject matter. Did Abba record a song that can sum up our Brexit mood?

Anyway, in the meantime, here's Peter and Linda so in future, you'll have the language to express your sensory overload:

Even though Steven has been home for nearly two years now, I still get an emotional reaction when he suddenly tells me a story about his life during the year at the positive behaviour unit. The stories that choke me up often have the same theme: Steven trying to communicate something but being ignored.

I've written before how Steven has signature tunes or signature sayings for most people in his life. At the Mencap pool, he always greets Dave with a quick chorus of "Heartbeat". One of the old cab drivers who used to take him to his water aerobics group would be serenaded with "I Will Do Anything For Love But I Won't Do That". I could give many examples of this type of communication.

This afternoon we were having a music session and I played "Sloop John B" by The Beach Boys. It turned out that whenever one of the male workers at the unit was on shift, Steven would greet him with: "I feel so broke up. I want to go home". Steven calls this his "Brian Wilson singing to Keith" (names have been changed to protect the guilty!)

Of course, it had long been decided by the professionals that Steven lacked capacity to decide where he should live but as the IMCA pointed out, that doesn't stop him having and expressing an opinion, or stating his wish. I've read the reports – if this sort of communication was acknowledged at all, which it rarely was, it was dismissed as an example of Steven's "repetitive speech patterns".

I'm pretty sure that the hundreds of logs I received logging Steven hitting out or throwing something, hid this kind of ignored communication. There was never any point in challenging it but I started to assume that at least some of the "incidents" must have followed times when he didn't feel listened to. Needless to say, that sort of valuable information was never recorded in any of the reports.

It's easier to play deaf.

The Casting Of Cats

It's 1969. I'm in the school playground and a group of friends and I are preparing to act out last night's episode of Please Sir. It's a weekly event. Knowing that I'm not hard enough to be Eric Duffy, I set my sights on being cast as Peter Craven, the cool guy with the very nice shirts. After much executive discussion, the general consensus is that I should play Dennis Dunstable, the loveable loser. Not on your nelly. I stomp off and refuse to share my bag of kola cubes until I'm recast. I'm not, so I eat all the kola cubes myself.

Fast forward some 35 years and today, Steven and his support worker are having a Cats session. Steven played The Rum Tum Tigger in the school Christmas show 2000. He could understudy any part as he knows all the lines. They are both singing their hearts out. I'm in the kitchen, cleaning the oven and I can tell that Steven is starting to get a bit cheesed off. His singing starts to have a slight divaish edge to it.

Eventually:

"You're a brown man Alan. You must be Old Deuteronemy. Steven Neary's Grissabella Cat".

I poke my head round the door and the support worker is trying to get into role as he sits down on the sofa, all wise and fatherly looking.

Taking centre stage, Steven falls theatrically to the floor, before getting up for his big chorus:

"Touch me. It's so easy to leave me. All alone with my memory......"

I could never negotiate the Peter Craven role but Steven manages to secure the Elaine Page part.

There must be a moral to this story.

Silly DoLS Talking

June 9, 2018

After 16 months of assessments, changes of social workers, endless paperwork, yesterday I finally got the completed paper work for the Community DoLS. I've written at length about the process before and hopefully, this will be the last post on the matter.

As a quick reminder, the concept of Community DoLS came about as a result of Lady Hale's acid test ruling in the Cheshire West Supreme Court appeal. A person is now deemed as being deprived of their liberty, regardless of where they live, as long as they meet the two acid drops of the acid test – are they free to leave and are they under constant supervision? If they aren't free to leave their own home and are under constant supervision then they are being deprived of their liberty. That kicks in those two lengthy and cumbersome processes: the mental capacity assessment and the best interests decision.

In Steven's case, the mental capacity assessment has been the most time consuming. For ages, the big question that nobody seemed to be able to answer was: does he have or lack the capacity to do what? In the end, having decided that it was the very substance of Steven's care arrangements: the 24/7 support in the home and the 2:1 support when he goes out that was the deprivation of his liberty, the focus of the capacity assessment became "does he have the capacity to consent to his care arrangements?". If the answer turned out to be that he lacks capacity in this area then the professionals would have to make a decision as to whether it is in his best interests to have these care arrangements and whether they were the least restrictive for his care. Considering they had already agreed to the care plan long before the Community DoLS appeared in the ballgame, the second aspect of the process seemed to be a foregone conclusion to me.

Are you keeping up? Have you got the capacity to take all this in? It could be you one day!

So, the paperwork has been completed and the bottom line of the assessments are that they have decided that Steven lacks the capacity to consent to his support arrangements but it is in his best interests and the least restrictive option for his care to have those support arrangements in place. Through the acid test lens, the very stuff that gives Steven his liberty is now seen as depriving him of it and the paperwork will shortly go to the Court of Protection for its authorisation.

I've already tweeted several of the highlights/lowlights of the report but I feel they deserve greater analysis as this is the process that every learning disabled person in the country will be going through at some point in the near future (if they already haven't done). I want to say that I'm not knocking the capacity assessor or the best interests assessor at all. They were tasked with an impossible mission. They were both meeting Steven for the first time. They were allocated about an hour to do the interviews. They were just pawns in this very silly game. And at the end of the day, they did both arrive at the only conclusion they could have done under these circumstances.

But. The assessments and outcome say nothing about Steven at all. He has so much more going for him than either assessor was able to elicit. Anybody that knows Steven will read the assessment and despair at how so many points were missed to really engage with him and would have given him and evens chance to display his understanding and wisdom. The fact that the assessments sail right pass the real Steven is no comment on him at all.

Here are some direct quotes from the report with my thoughts:

"I asked 'Where do you live?' Steven said 'Cowley House' and pointed at the floor. I then asked him where is Cowley near? Despite offering this question a few times, Steven repeated his previous statement".

Okay, Steven was able to say where he lives. I don't understand what the question about where is Cowley near has got to do with anything. Does geography come into a mental capacity assessment? Steven knows that his house is near to Uncle Wayne's and Jay's sweet shop but I don't think he would have answered that from the way the question was phrased. Has being able to judge distance got much to do with demonstrating your mental capacity?

"I asked Steven if he lived with other people. Steven said yes. I asked who these people were. Steven said "Mark Neary and Des and Alan and Chris Young. I asked Steven 'who cares for you?' to see if I could help him make a distinction between these two concepts. Steven mentioned many of the same people above. I repeated the question and Steven repeated his response".

What is the correct answer? Those people do live with Steven, in his eyes. They eat and sleep in Steven's house during the week. Steven is remarkably comfortable in his own skin and doesn't see himself as dependent on others.

He certainly doesn't carry the emotional baggage that people carry when they need to rely on others for support. To him, life is much more straight forward – these are people in my life who I do things with.

"I asked who takes Steven swimming. He said 'Michael and Alan'. I asked Steven whether he would be safe to go swimming by himself. He said 'no'. I repeated this question and he said 'yes'".

He gave the correct answer. He does go swimming with Michael and Alan and he knows that he can't go by himself. Asking the question is dodgy psychology. Steven is very eager to please. He probably assumed that he had got the answer wrong first time and was being given a second stab at it. I dunno but that strikes me as a little cruel.

"We talked about cookery. Steven gave me the answer first that he cooked his meals and when I asked him a second time he said that staff did so. The support staff pointed out that both are true; Steven is able to use the microwave by himself but freshly prepared meals are made by staff".

Thank goodness that the support workers were able to point this out. Without their intervention Steven's reply would have been filed away in that category of not understanding the question.

"We talked about what Steven would do if there was a fire in the house. Steven became distressed at the idea of a fire and did not pay heed to my question about what he might do in such an instance. I moved on from this questioning after reassuring Steven that there was no fire in the house at the moment".

This one seriously pisses me off. For two reasons. I accept that the assessor couldn't have foreseen that his question would have caused distress. The fact that he mentions it in his report suggests though that he still doesn't realise that it was his questioning that caused the distress. Steven does know what to do in the event of a fire. Anyone with even a tiny knowledge of him will know that he follows the Basil Fawlty procedure to fire safety. Many years ago we were on holiday in a caravan. It had a gas cooker which we had never used before. I was outside on the sun lounger one afternoon when I heard him shout: "Fire. Fire. Everybody out now please" and he proceeded to lead Julie by the hand out of the caravan. He thought the gas ring was on fire and demonstrated that he knew the premises needed to be evacuated. But of course, when you take your life cues from Basil and Mr Bean, you're hardly likely to be seen as such during a mental capacity assessment.

"I showed Steven a picture of bleach and cleaning products. I asked Steven to identify them and he said 'soap'. I asked Steven who used them in the house and he said 'Des'. I asked Steven if he used them and he gave different answers on the first and second occasions I asked".

Again, Steven gave the correct answer. Des bleaches the kitchen floor every Monday afternoon whilst Steven is watching his DVD. And another example of asking the same question more than once. It just seems destined to trip the person up.

At this point in the assessment, the assessor returned to earlier themes. Steven slips into echolalia. To me and the support team we know that is a sign that Steven is tired or tense or both.

"I asked about going out – again he told me who took him but did not respond when I asked if he was safe to go out alone – repeating my question back to me".

Tortuous, isn't it?

Then came the first bit of humanity during the whole assessment. Thank goodness we've got Des on our team:

"I asked the support workers whether there was any other way I could communicate these questions. Des said that Steven understood much of what i was saying but that I wasn't giving him enough processing time".

I cried when I read that paragraph. Thank you Des. He's right. It can take Steven a couple of hours, a couple of days, a couple of months to process stuff. Putting pressure on him or trying to trip him up isn't going to speed up his processing time and ability.

The final paragraph reads:

"Whilst Steven seemed to indicate that he was happy with his care and support and his home, he did not understand the information relevant to the decision which he would need to weigh to make a decision to the question at hand".

Does that make sense to anyone? It's very clumsily phrased. Whatever it means, it feels like the whole assessment was geared to produce that outcome.

There's been some very supportive feedback on social media. This from Rob Mitchell:

"The failure is that the assessor hasn't enabled Steven as per Principle 2. A series of questions aimed at catching him out, proving incapacity, ticking the box, keeping Steven in his place & moving on."

And this from Dicky Biscuit:

"It's the BIA's skills at communication being tested not the P's. Considering the power imbalance betwen P and the BIA, BIA asks a question and gets an answer. BIA asks question again (Why??). P, unsure if 1st answer displeased BIA, gives a different answer. BIA finds incapacity."

In a year's time the whole thing will start all over again. I imagine that Steven won't see either assessor before then so any chance of building a relationship and getting a better understanding of how he operates won't happen.

I was discussing the report with the support worker this afternoon and we were both unhappy with two references within the report to Steven becoming "distressed". How can we make this silly process less distressing for him next time? The truth is we can't.

Steven heard us talking and wanted to know more. I was at a loss. And then true to form, Steven came to my aid. He dismissed what I was saying as "silly talking". That gave me the idea. Next year we'll say: "A man is coming this afternoon to play a silly game and do some silly talking". He can cope with that. It should take some of the tension away. We had to explain Gladiators to him in much the same way when he got worried that Hunter was really trying to take the contender's head off with his pugel stick. It's not real. It's a silly game. Just like a Community DoLS.

Only I know that it is real. It's abusive. It's disrespectful. And it's the type of practice that leads directly to the way learning disabled people are treated as horrifically presented in the #LeDeR report.

But who gives a toss when there's paperwork to be done.

I Don't Want A Horse

February 17, 2013

On Friday, I received the cheque for Steven's damages award. I defy anyone who receives an unexpected lump sum not to consider a treat. This is how the conversation went:

Me: "Steve – would you like a big surprise for your birthday?" (I knew this was too vague a question)

Steve: "A BIG surprise? A BIG one? I don't want a horse".

Me: "No, not a horse. Would you like a special treat? Do you want to go and see a show?"

Steve: "Seen Grease. Seen Blood Brothers. No, not a show"

Me: "Would you like to go on a holiday for your birthday?"

Steve: (laughing) A holiday in March. Dad's doing silly talking.

Me: "No. We can have a birthday holiday and a summer holiday"

Steve: "That's a bit greedy. Center Parcs in March?"

Me: "We can go to Center Parcs in March. Shall we go to Center Parcs in March?"

Steve: (Getting very excited) Yes. Phone Uncle Wayne and tell him we're going to Center Parcs".

So, Center Parcs it is then. This was one of the things on Steven's person centred plan wish list in 2010 that was refused by the positive behaviour unit. He's always wanted to go there since he was about seven and saw pictures of his two cousins there.

Measurable Outcomes & Brookside

One thing that all families with a learning disabled member learns very early on is that when you ask for services you have to enter the professionals' world. They don't enter yours. Your life becomes framed and narrated in a way that you have never done before. It is expected that you learn the language and the processes. If you don't, you're in completely alien territory even though that territory is your life.

You are led to think in terms of tasks, of measurable outcomes, of action plans. It's a business speak that is very hard to fit with the way you live your life.

I remember a story from the time Steven was in the Unit. I had to attend an update review meeting about two months after Steven was detained. One thing I brought up was Steven's clothes. All the ones he went away with had either been lost, damaged or shrunk beyond wearing. It was tense because the professionals went on the defensive. We had a long discussion about replacements and I offered to order a new wardrobe that evening & Steven would have the new clothes by the weekend. A few days later I was sent an "action plan" resulting from the meeting. One paragraph was:

"Task – To buy new clothes for SN".

"Tasked to – MN"

"Completion Date – 26.2.10"

"Outcome – To improve SN's choice of clothing".

A normal everyday job that didn't even merit recording was turned into corporate cobblers.

For years after Steven transitioned into adult services (I can speak the lingo) I was asked when I saw the time when Steven would be living independently. A major life development had to be reduced to a "task, completion and outcome" box. I could never answer the question in a way that I was expected to. I'd mumble something like, "Well, I'm sure it will happen when it happens. When Steven is ready". I knew it was the wrong answer although it was the only right answer I could envisage. I knew I was right because Steven's whole life had progressed like that. He learns things when he's ready to learn them.

Today is a perfect, albeit minor example of this. Earlier I told Steven about an episode of Morse that I thought he might be interested in that was being repeated on ITV3 this afternoon. To coin a phrase, "They're all in it". Lots of actors that Steven would recognise from other shows. He likes that when familiar faces turn up in other shows. I gave him some clues:

"The man from One Foot In The Grave & Mr Bean's dentist".

(Easy peasy) " Richard Wilson? And?"

"That naughty man from Brookside".

"Robert Pugh".

Good grief! He didn't say John Clarke. Clarke was the character in Brookside who held the nurses hostage back in 1984, finally shooting Kate and then himself. Steven has watched the video many times and can quote many of the lines.

But he knew the actor's name and that he was playing a part. It's the first time he's differentiated between an actor and the part he plays.

It's taken 27 1/2 years. Perhaps, he's known that for years and hasn't been able to articulate it before. Who knows? Whatever, he's done it in his own time without any recourse to an action plan.

That's how we live our lives.

April 26, 2013

Sometimes, my son can be a genius.

Two weeks ago, Steven had his mental capacity assessment to determine if he had the capacity to manage a tenancy. It was carried out by his social worker, who we shall call Dusty (the relevance of that should become obvious). She did the assessment in two stages: Part one was a series of questions around tenancies to check his level of understanding; Part two, was two days later, and assessed if he'd been able to retain the information from part one. I've not yet been told the outcome but as the assessment was contrived to give the council more clout to pursue their main agenda (making Steven the tenant of our property and usurping my position as his property and affairs deputy), I guess the outcome is a foregone conclusion.

Last night we were having a music DVD session. This is a regular Thursday night event: 20 music tracks by a wide variety of artists. Whilst watching one track, Steven became very excited and animated:

"Dusty was talking about The Pet Shop Boys".

I didn't get what he was on about at first but he kept repeating himself and pointing at the screen. We were watching The Pet Shop Boys performing "Rent". I got it. Dusty must have asked Steven about rent during the mental capacity assessment.

Margi Clarke appears in the video and whenever we watch it, Steven is always intrigued whether Margi lives with Neil Tenant or Chris Lowe. As the video ends with Margi and Chris having a cuddle on Paddington Station, we assume it's the latter. But as usual, Steven wanted to confirm that Margi Clarke lives with Chris Lowe.

And having sorted that question out, he then said:

"Margi Clarke gives money to Chris Lowe".

He couldn't explain any more than that but it can only really mean one thing. There is no other reason why Margi should be giving money to Chris Lowe. Steven must have worked out that if she lives with Mr Lowe, then Margi must be giving him money for rent.

If I'm right, and I'm sure that I am, that must mean that he understands that rent is something you pay for living somewhere. Isn't that brilliant.

The sad thing is there is absolutely no point in telling that story to social services. They have always dismissed Steven's ability to communicate a strong message through song. But also, as I said above, it muddies the water of their main intention. The assessment was a contrivance for another agenda. It's like 2010 all over again.

The first line of "Rent" is: "You dress me up – I'm your puppet".

I know how it feels.

Be Happy Audrey. I Say, Be Happy

Steven and I used to have running joke about his echolalia – he used to call it "talking like Fred Elliott". Steven likes me doing impressions and one of his favourites is the genial Coronation Street butcher's last words: "Be happy Audrey. I say, be happy". It was a poignant scene. So, in the past when we have been in important assessments or professional's meetings and I can see Steven getting worked up and slipping into echolalia, I say: "Steven's doing his.....?" and he replies, "Steven's doing his Fred Elliott talking". And he laughs and the anxiety is dissolved.

My My, DoLS Meet Their Waterloo

WARNING

This post contains some distressing images of a person being deprived of their liberty.

On Friday, we chose the least restrictive option for Steven's care (There was only a celebrity Storage Hunters special on the telly) and spent the evening in the company of a counterfeit Agnetha, Anna Frid, Bjorn and Benny.

We lived dangerously because we didn't get this deprivation authorised but Steven did demonstrate his capacity by inviting me to tag along.

The conditions we attached to this DoLS was to sing and dance and clap as loudly as possible.

We achieved those conditions.

Soundtrack To A Birth

March 18, 2015

A few years ago for Steven's birthday, I did a compilation tape of songs that had been at number one on his birthday. Every year, he makes me do the same tape and he listens to it on the day before his birthday.

He's playing it now and the annual narrative has completely floored his support worker. Steven is especially keen on the song from his actual birth date – Dub Be Good To Me by Beats International. The commentary is the same every year:

"Here comes Steven Neary.

Steven Neary is not a seed anymore.

Steven Neary is coming out of mummy's fanny.

Mummy is shouting and holding daddy's hand.

Steven Neary is in the world now.

Nice to meet you Steven Neary.

Hello Norman Cook".

A Painful Pathway

February 11, 2017

Steven had a bit of a shock last night at the Mencap Pool. There was a first timer there; a guy probably a few years younger than him with a carer.

Steven can be thoroughly ruthless with other learning disabled people – they almost become invisible to him. But he is very interested in the carers.

So he swam over to the new chap's carer and did his usual; "Hello man. What's your name man?"

The carer replied: "Oh come on Steven. You know my name. You know who I am".

Steven got right up close to the chap's face before delightedly exclaiming: "It's John from M".

It was one of the guys who used to work at the respite place Steven went to for about a year. The place that Steven has been too scared to go back to since he was released from his detention. It's the place where he went for one night in 2009 before Whistler's Mother dragged him off to the Positive Behaviour Unit.

When Steven was telling me about the encounter he became concerned for the young lad who was there with John. Let's call him Alfie.

"Alfie will be going to M House for a long time. Alfie can't go to his Mum and Dad's house for a massive long time. Alfie will be sad".

Steven has obviously got it into his head that anyone who goes to the respite place are automatically on a conveyor belt to the positive behaviour unit.

Who knows? He may be right. Since 2010, I've met several people locally for whom the care pathways in Hillingdon are absolutely terrifying.

It's A "Thing" Word

Steven doesn't really do adjectives.

He has a couple. "Massive" is one. As in "Steven's done a massive blow off" or "Meat Loaf's got a massive belly".

The other one is: "a little bit". As in "Steven's done a little bit blow off", or "Got a little bit silly head on today".

Now we can add a third. The other day whilst listening to Phil Collins singing a Groovy Kind of Love, Steven asked:

"Dad, groovy is a ....?"

"Ummm. Groovy is a....."

"Groovy is a thing?"

"Groovy means great. Or fantastic. Or excellent".

"Woody's got a groovy hat?"

"Yeah. That's what groovy means"

"Paul Heaton does groovy singing?"

"Yeah. That's groovy as well".

So, in the Cowley house, it's become the word of the summer.

Yesterday, I got home from work and Steven told me about his afternoon. He had been watching a 4 hour video of Graham Norton presenting the 100 Greatest Number One hits of all time.

"That was a massive video Steve"

"It was a massive, groovy video Dad".

You wait 24 years for an adjective and then two come along at once.

Expertise

March 29, 2017

Another day. Another Twitter debate about why thousands of people are trapped in ATUs. Another debate where professionals who should know better pull out their trump card – "Lack of local expertise and skills" to shut down the real truth – lack of will and vested interests – being exposed.

I'm too fed up with that tired, offensive excuse being trotted out with depressing regularity. The implication stinks – the person is too complicated and challenging to be living in their own home and an institution is the best place for them. Engaging in that conversation perpetuates the fantasy, so let's stop doing it.

Instead, let me tell you a few things that have happened in Cowley over the past fortnight and the input of Steven's "unskilled, inexpert support team".

1. Brought and fitted new living room curtains after a meltdown led to the slat blinds lying in a crumpled heap on the floor.

2. Taught Steven what the African lyrics in Going Back To My Roots mean.

3. Sat for an hour on Steven's bed, reassuring him when he was upset and anxious about my late return from Scunthorpe.

4. Extended a shift by 45 minutes (unpaid) to go to the shop to buy some Crumbled ham.

5. Upon delivery of his new CD, learned and discussed the difference between Laurence Fox and Mr James Hathaway.

6. Took a pair of pyjamas with a hole in the crutch, home to repair.

7. Noticed the small sweet shop was busy and waited outside singing Shania Twain songs until the shop cleared.

8. Discovered a TV channel that plays 1980s music videos 24/7.

9. Mowed the back lawn.

10. Rearranged Steven's schedule when they realised Take That were appearing on the Ant & Dec show.

That's the sort of skilled expertise that's developed when you have human beings interested in each other.

Uxbridge Evacuates

October 1, 2013

We live in a privately rented 2 bedroom flat in a small block. From our kitchen window, you can see directly into the windows of the three kitchens opposite. Steven had the occupants all sussed within a few days of our moving in.

From left flat to right flat we have: Nelson Mandela, who always looked slightly startled when he bumps into Steven who greets him with – "Nice to see you Nelson Mandela, to see you nice".

The middle flat is a guy called Pete. Steven learned over time that his name was Pete but stuck with his original naming of him – John Suchet's brother.

The flat on the right has had a variety of students but one constant has been – Elvis Costello – a geeky looking but game chap who after about a year decided that it was best to join in when Steven serenaded him with "Oliver's Army".

Across the landing from us is a lovely family, headed by Diego, who surprisingly has remained just Diego. Steven likes Diego, who lets him stroke his motorbike.

And downstairs have been a succession of tenants who only seem to last a year, perhaps pissed off by our leaking radiator, that the landlady has never fixed, dribbling down their wall. The last tenant was Richard Madeley.

Since the summer, one by one, all the old faces have left the Close. Nelson Mandela was the first to go and Steven refuses to believe that he has actually left, instead concocting a story of Nelson hurting his back and having to have a long lay down on his sofa. Whilst we were on holiday, Richard Madeley left and John Suchet's brother followed soon after. We had a bad time on Sunday, when Steven noticed Elvis packing all of his belongings into a van. And bugger me, whilst browsing an estate agent's window this morning, I saw that Diego's flat is up for sale.

Yep. After a year of stress because we haven't known if we're coming or going, we're the only ones left. The last men standing.

Printed in Great Britain
by Amazon